THE LADIES AREN'T FOR SILENCE!
(Gentlemen are you listening?)

THE LADIES AREN'T FOR SILENCE!
(Gentlemen are you listening?)

Foreword by John Noble
Conclusion by Dave Tomlinson
Written and Edited by Joan Martin

WORD PUBLISHING

Word (UK) Ltd
Milton Keynes, England

WORD AUSTRALIA
Kilsyth, Victoria, Australia

WORD COMMUNICATIONS LTD
Vancouver, B.C., Canada

STRUIK CHRISTIAN BOOKS (PTY) LTD
Maitland, South Africa

ALBY COMMERCIAL ENTERPRISES PTE LTD
Balmoral Road, Singapore

CHRISTIAN MARKETING NEW ZEALAND LTD
Havelock North, New Zealand

JENSCO LTD
Hong Kong

SALVATION BOOK CENTRE
Malaysia

THE LADIES AREN'T FOR SILENCE
(Gentlemen are you listening?)

ISBN 0-85009-234-5 (Australia 1-86258-153-3)

All Scripture quotations unless otherwise stated are from the New
International Version © 1978 International Bible Society, New York.

Quotations on p. 33 from Tertullian, *On the Apparel of Women* in *The
Church Fathers*, ed. Roberts and Donaldson (1951), and on p. 162
from Jewett, P.K., *Man as Male and Female* (1975) by permission of
Wm. B. Eerdmans Publishing Co.

Quotations on p.113 from Gladwin, J., *God's People in God's World*
(1979), on pp. 166 and 170 from *The New Bible Dictionary*, 2nd Edn.
(1982, ed. N. Hillyer) and on p. 163 from Milne, B., *Know The Truth*
(1982) by permission of Inter-Varsity Press.

Quotation on pp. 59 and 66 from Bilezikian, G., *Beyond Sex Roles*
(1985), and on p. 170 from McPheeters, J.C., *Proclaiming The New
Testament: The Epistles To The Corinthians* (1964) by permission of Baker
Book House.

Quotation on p. 162 from Langley, M., *Equal Woman* (1983) by
permission of Harper Collins.

Quotations on pp. 170 and 172 from Atkins, A., *Split Image* (1987)
by permission of Hodder and Stoughton.

Quotations on p. 75 from Storkey, E., *What's Right With Feminism*
(1985) and on pp. 226, 231, 233 and 234 from Hayter, M., *The New
Eve in Christ* (1982) by permission of SPCK.

Quotation on p. 168 from Gundry, P., *Woman Be Free* (Zondervan,
1977) — permission applied for.

Quotation on pp. 169-170 from De Vaux, R., *Ancient Israel — Its Life
and Institutions* (1980) by permission of Darton, Longman and Todd.

Typesetting by Phoenix Manor, Milton Keynes.
Reproduced, printed and bound in Great Britain for Word (UK) Ltd
by Richard Clay Ltd., Bungay, Suffolk.

91 92 93 94 / 10 9 8 7 6 5 4 3 2 1

Acknowledgements

My thanks are due firstly to my husband Daryl, without whose love, patience and ability in grammatical English this book would not have been written. His was the initial idea or seed thought. He was indeed the 'source' of my life, in this venture!

Secondly, my thanks are due to my children Debbie, Jonathan, Mandy, Ruth, Sheila and Clare, who gave Mum time and extra time so often in the past three years.

Thirdly, to all my friends in the family of God locally and nationally, who by their friendship have put into me those things that I needed to work this project through. Particularly I want to thank Christine Noble who helped with the questions and encouraged me yet again to 'go for it'.

My thanks are also due to John Noble for his Foreword and his encouragement to me and to Dave Tomlinson for his searching and exciting Conclusion, and for the hours of typing given me freely particularly by Fred, and Wendy and Mary, whose ideas helped me with the title.

Finally, and most importantly, my heartfelt thanks to every lady in this book. As I have worked on it, I do feel that you have all become my friends, in a special way. Thank you for your encouragement and trust. Without you this would never have been written.

In all these things — I give thanks to Him.

Contents

FOREWORD

The Breakdown of the Patriarchal Society

Spirit-filled Christians have to learn to live with joy and frustration — joy because the kingdom has come and frustration because it's not yet here. We already have one foot firmly planted in heaven since we have stepped upward, lifted by Christ's royal law of love. Nevertheless, our physical bodies keep us tied to a world marred and tainted with sin. We have caught a glimpse of a new age where the diversions and limitations of class, race and sex are eliminated, but we still wrestle with injustice and unrighteousness which abound everywhere.

Today as we approach the end of this present age, the whole of creation is groaning and travailing, longing to break free from the bondage which the Fall brought upon us. Man inwardly knows he was made to rule and have authority and struggles against his slavery to the earth, his fellow men and the principalities and powers, which presently oversee the world. This struggle can be seen both within the Church and also in the world at large as mankind comes to maturity.

The patriarchal system, instituted by God after the Fall, was given as a part of the curse and was intended to maintain order until the 'seed' of the woman overcame Satan. It provided us with some kind of social structure to hold a rebellious creation in check until the work of salvation was complete. Those who accept the atoning sacrifice of Jesus are set free from slavery of all kinds. Thus in Christ there is no bond or free, no black or white, no male or female. As the harvest of good and evil grow up side by side waiting for the final ingathering, we can observe the efforts of those in darkness to overthrow the old patriarchal system by violence, rebellion and militancy. And they are not without success, for the old order is crumbling all around us and at all levels in our society.

Christians know that freedom cannot be grasped or gained by human effort. The Devil's 'new age' movement, designed to bring man to full consciousness, is doomed to failure as it is based on pride, arrogance and deception. For us freedom comes only by acknowledging the Lordship of Jesus and living by the priorities of truth, love, forgiveness and mutual submission. In this way earthly structures become redundant as we learn to live in honesty and peace. The visible evidence of our new kingdom life will be seen in the way Christian employers and employees relate. It will be manifest in racial harmony amongst us and in the way in which men and women can work and function together.

In the midst of all the upheaval going on in our world, there are many encouraging signs in the Church. One of these is the way in which more and more women are able to express themselves and take up their rightful place alongside the men without infighting or conflict. This is a work of the Holy Spirit.

In completing this book, Joan Martin has produced a remarkable achievement. She has not only tracked down a number of her women from a wide range of backgrounds, experiences and traditions, but has also managed to get them to talk and share their feelings with us. To accomplish this, when all these ladies are leading extremely busy lives, is not far short of a miracle. We should appreciate all the more the valuable insights and encouragements which they give. Joan has not attempted to hide the fact that they are not able to dot one another's theological 'i's or cross one another's doctrinal 't's, but her work reveals one common point of agreement. It is time for all men and women of God to function at full throttle as the work of the kingdom needs every one of us released, to serve our worthy Saviour and His cause. Thank you Joan, and thank you ladies.

John Noble

Introduction

For the past fifteen years in the Church, God has been speaking to many of us about men and women's relationships and roles. This has been particularly within the area of the social order concerning husbands, wives, the family including children, and singles within the context of extended families.

Today many of us find ourselves asking questions on the role of women within the Church, in the context of church order rather than social order. This is not a book about the ordination of women nor about whether women should wear hats or headcoverings in church. Its aim is not to be contentious.

My burden is one that has grown over the recent past, when in counselling situations I have seen women locked into the syndrome of 'wife and mother roles', feeling there is nothing else for them in the Church. These women have been called 'God's frozen assets', with gifts and ministries locked away that need releasing.

My burden starts here, but also goes on to see that God also wants some women today, as in the New Testament, named amongst the brethren. They were named because they were leading in gifts and ministry. This was not to be in isolation, but as part — an essential part — of the team.

To that end, I have asked some of those women already moving out to encourage the rest of us, by sharing the steps they have taken and are taking to overcome the issues they have had to face in their lives. In interviewing them, I used a set of ten basic questions, which form the basis of the ten main chapters of this book.

The questions are as follows:

1. In the eyes of God, ''Am I a person in my own right, and if I am does this mean that I can have a personal

ministry?''
2. What do you think about 'feminism' today?
3. What do you feel about the submission of women to men (plural), in comparison to ''Wives submit to your husbands'', as in Ephesians 5:22? What does it mean?
4. It is often quoted that women are more open to deception than men. How do you feel about this in the light of the fact that most of the large sects were started by men, e.g. Mormons, Jehovah's Witnesses, Moonies, etc.?
5. How have you overcome the attitude that ''I must be wrong'', after feeling the intuitive check or 'clunk' over a matter that a woman so often feels?
6. What do you feel Paul means by saying it is better to be single than married, in 1 Corinthians 7:8? How would you view yourself, if you had not chosen to be married? What would your *raison d'etre* be, knowing your position in leadership now? For example, might you have become a woman in authority on the mission field?
7. What do you feel about the issue of home versus career?
8. How much should women be involved in social concerns like: women's refuge work, battered wives and battered children?
9. What do you feel about women in leadership?
10. As a woman in leadership, how are you leading those who are following after you?

Not every lady totally agrees with every other lady on every detail, at this moment in time, as can be seen. However, there is a consensus of opinion running through all the answers to these questions. It is very interesting to see that God has been leading so many in a similar direction. The time is short and the need is great.

We can all take encouragement from the fact that God is calling His women out into their gifts and ministries, which He has created us for, and that He is calling some into positions of leadership, unthought of a few years ago. More than this, we can also see that what is really on God's heart is not so much that women alone should now move out, but rather that women and men together should see the kingdom of God built as they begin to move together in partnership.

Gentlemen too are questioning the status quo. A well-known Christian leader was recently heard to say, at a Christian conference, that there was male apartheid in the Church. He stated that many men in the Church had voted for Margaret Thatcher to lead Britain, but they would not allow her to speak in their church! So it is apparent that many questions need answering.

During the writing of this book, there have been times of real struggle — times of illness and surgery; death in the family and financial crisis. The house was struck by lightning. It seemed as though the blue streak passed from the open window next to me, between my face and my tape machine, as I worked on these interviews, before it finally blew up the television set which my son was watching. A young 'punk' living with us returned to her roots, which included Satanism. God has also protected us from flood, earthquake and a hurricane. We adopted four little girls into our family. Yet through all this and much more I have consistently heard the Lord saying about this project, as I have struggled to continue, ''Keep on, keep pushing the door.'' I trust that He will use the thoughts of all these people to accomplish what is on His heart for women and men together in the Church today.

Who's Who?

SYLVIA MARY ALISON

Sylvia Mary was born in Brazil. Her father was a diplomat. She came to London at the age of sixteen, when her father moved to work in the Foreign Office. In 1954, she was converted at a Billy Graham rally at Harringay. After gaining three A levels, she went to the London School of Economics, gained a Social Science Certificate, then worked for two years as a social therapist in a unit attached to a mental hospital.

Sylvia Mary married Michael in 1958, and their three children James, Sebastian and Mary Rose were born in 1959, 1961 and 1964. In 1964 Michael became an MP for a Yorkshire constituency. This has meant a difficult life style, with many evenings alone for Sylvia Mary. But in all that God has worked His purposes out and ever since their marriage Sylvia Mary has been involved in Christian groups, such as the Parliamentary Wives group, and has held such positions as Chairman of the Prayer Committee for Spree '73.

In the late seventies she was involved in the Nationwide Initiative on Evangelism, and Prison Fellowship was born in 1978, after she had held the vision in her heart for almost twenty years. Sylvia Mary knew God was calling her to work in prisons soon after her conversion. Her book *God is Building a House* was published in 1984. This describes further the vision and history of Prison Fellowship, and how God has led her through her Christian life. Today she is involved in several areas of Christian work, and she and Michael worship regularly at an Anglican church.

ROSEMARY ANDREWS

Rosemary was born in Poole, Dorset in 1941. She grew up in an atmosphere of hostility, aggression and violence, becoming very withdrawn, isolated and full of fear. Being aware of God at an early age, she went to Sunday School, but there they said she was rebellious. Her reactions were probably those of someone who could not receive any love because she felt so rejected.

The constant tension at home made her unhappy and unable to concentrate at school. Inferiority crept into her life because her father would not use money to buy new clothes and second-hand ones were the norm. She isolated herself in books and escaped into worlds of adventure and romance. At seventeen and a half she left home to pursue a nursing career, without discussing it with her father.

Going into the world was traumatic. Rosemary would submit to everybody. She had never had a chance in life to choose or discuss anything. Her life became one round of parties, which was a relief from the long hours on the wards. She enjoyed nursing people, but was very afraid of matrons, sisters and doctors and would become very dithery and self-conscious in their presence.

She met Ian at a dance and a couple of years later they were married. Later she was asked to go to Westminster Chapel in London by a friend. Rosemary and Ian went for some months until they were pressed to make a decision as to whether to believe the claims of Jesus Christ. In a very calm way they decided to become Christians. Then having tried to be good Christians for some time, they found they were pretty hopeless at it!

In 1967 they were invited to a fellowship in Chard. Rosemary was convicted and challenged hearing an old tape about people being healed. Never having been able to communicate, being tongue-tied and full of fear, she understood that her fears of a big hard God came from a concept of Dad that was totally unfounded. She decided to let Jesus be her Lord, but told Him that she wanted an experience like those in the Bible. Jesus appeared to her in the room. She saw Him look into her eyes telling her that

He could find no fault in her. She knew that she was accepted. Waves of love and joy filled her. Rejection and anger left.

With little knowledge and training in how to help people, she began, with Ian, to give this new life away. They had a home full of people and ministered to all who came. Even if people brought their sick dogs, they got prayed for too! Six months after moving to Chard, Ian was made redundant and they began to live by faith. They embarked on a full-time ministry. They had words to confirm that God had called them as individuals and as a husband and wife together. Ian and Rosemary now travel together and minister to many nationwide and abroad.

GRACE BARNES

Grace has always lived on the east side of London. She was born in Whitechapel Road in 1935. She is aware that God has had His hand on her life from the time she was born. The doctor told her mother that Grace would probably not be born alive. When she was, the doctor said her name should be Grace, because she was a gift of God.

Coming from a religious background, at the age of eleven she came into her own experience of Christ. At thirteen she belonged to a children's Bible class; a friend had a vision of Africa, and knew that God had called her into the mission field. Grace had recently been baptised in the Holy Spirit, and wanted to know what she could do. God spoke to her clearly, saying that she would marry an evangelist, and that she would live out of a suitcase!

Norman's Mum saw Grace walk into the church one day and decided that she was the right wife for her son! Grace and Norman did not know about this until after they were married. Not long after this, John Noble, a friend, rang up and asked Norman to speak at a Shaftesbury Mission in Chadwell Heath, East London, a little mission with a dozen people in it. Norman and Grace were eventually asked to lead this work. Norman freely admits that although he gets most of the credit for the growth of the work, it was in fact Grace who was the real pastor.

After three years of marriage Grace became pregnant, having had a history of fibroids and operations. At four months, she lost the baby in a miscarriage. After several more operations, when she still hoped for a family, at forty-one she finally had to have a hysterectomy. God had asked her to lay down the possibility of having a family. Grace and Norman then asked God for a spiritual family, which He has given them.

God then began to speak to them on community life. One or two people moved in to live close by the Mission and Grace worked with elderly people and would regularly do their washing and give them dinners. As they grew very old, she would eventually sit with them while they died, and then wash and lay them out. She was definitely the pastor and Norman was the evangelist. Today they have an eldership team of which Grace is a part, and she has also become more involved in having input into other churches. She has organised a number of highly successful women's conferences and with Norman has written a book about their life and their international ministry through Links International.

SUE BARNETT

Sue was born in London and educated in South London. In 1960 she was trained in Eastbourne as a teacher and then taught in three London schools. She then met her husband Doug, who has been a full-time evangelist for over twenty-five years, latterly with the now well-known Saltmine Trust.

When her sons started school, she went back into teaching for a while. In her last post she felt God was calling her out of teaching into full-time ministry. Her ministry developed as her sons grew up and it is only in the past few years that she has been working in a full-time capacity with the Saltmine Trust, an international evangelistic team engaged in church-based missions. Married for twenty-four years, Sue and Doug have extended their family to include a 'daughter' who is in her thirties. They have an open home with many people coming and going.

Sue's first experience of God came in her teens. It is a

parallel experience to her experience of her earthly father.
For the first three years of her life, the name 'Daddy' was
only a name and a photograph. The trauma came when he
came home from the war, and she realised that he was alive.
The same thing happened with the name of Jesus. It was just
a name that meant presents at Christmas. In her teens the
mention of Jesus caused discomfort, with the gradual
realisation that Jesus was a living person who wanted a
relationship with her. From an early commitment has grown
a life-changing relationship, which particularly in the last few
years has proved God to be alive and powerful by His Spirit.
Sue has written a book on all-round fitness, called *Fit for a
King*, which she uses to share her faith as she speaks to
groups around the country.

REVD MYRA BLYTH

Myra was born in Larkhall near Glasgow. Her father was a
Baptist minister. When Myra was six, the family moved to
London, where her father worked at the headquarters,
involved in stewardship. She then remained in the south of
England, except for four years in Wales. Myra comes from
a very close family, where everything was shared. Mealtimes
were extremely intense, either full of hilarity or debate. This
made her fairly clear in her ideas and quite strong as a debater
and persuader.

She does not remember a time of not believing in God. At
the age of five she asked Christ to come into her life, but it
was not until the sixth form, when she changed one A Level
from Music to Scripture, that she suddenly found permission
to read the Bible in a new way which helped her faith to take
a leap. Myra trained for the ministry at Regents Park College
in London, and during the last decade has been working in
the ecumenical movement.

She has met Christians from many traditions such as the
Russian Orthodox Church and the Society of Friends. These
two traditions in particular have brought Myra a deeper
understanding of the doctrines of the Trinity and the
Incarnation, and a new awareness of the Eucharist and the
significance of the bread and wine respectively, that she did

not have from her own Baptist tradition. Myra has been married for thirteen years, she and her husband have chosen not to have children and they worship regularly in the church where Myra used to be an assistant minister.

GENERAL EVA BURROWS

General Eva Burrows was born in Australia, into a Salvation Army family. Her parents were dedicated Salvationists and both her mother and father were ordained. Her mother preached and was active in the ministry of the church, and being full of compassion, often brought home an extra person to join their meals. As there were nine children in the family, there was always room for another, and with a mother who was good at personal contact, Eva remembers that this was a regular occurrence! At her mother's funeral, the church was packed to the doors with people who had been touched significantly by her life.

In her teens Eva went through a period of rebellion against the family discipline. It was in her first year at university that she had a life-transforming experience of conversion. This was while she was at the Queensland University in Brisbane. At an IVF Youth Camp, studying Paul's letter to the Romans, she began to turn her whole thought towards Christ. The Salvation Army preach for a verdict, and so she made her commitment in a Salvation Army Youth Rally. An awareness of a call to the ministry also came and from there she was enrolled as a Salvation Army soldier, and has never looked back.

After gaining her degree, she trained for the ministry at the Salvation Army training college in London. She then went straight to Rhodesia (now Zimbabwe) in Africa as a missionary educator, where she stayed for seventeen years. Returning to London to the International College, she was first its Vice-Principal and then the Principal. Later still she served as Commander in Sri Lanka, then as Commander in Scotland, and finally as Commander in Australia, before she was elected to be General and world leader of the whole movement, which contains around two million people.

RUTH CALVER

Ruth and her husband Clive live hectic lives in South-East London, Clive working for the Evangelical Alliance, and Ruth running their home, caring for their children, working on the PTA, being a school governor and leading in the women's work in their local fellowship. Ruth was raised in a Christian home before going to Lebanon at nineteen to serve with VSO. During that time, Christmas 1968 to be exact, she found herself in the middle of an air raid, with the Israelis bombing Beirut Airport. Ruth was with Lebanese Christians who did not know whether or not their families were dying as the bombs fell. They were praising the Lord during the bombing. Ruth found she was terrified of dying and threw herself on the Lord. She found His peace in that situation when thirteen jets were destroyed above their heads.

That day had a major effect on Ruth's life. She had always enjoyed having a boyfriend of some sort and felt the Lord say clearly at that time that the next one was going to be the final one, if she would allow Him to direct her. She did not go out with anyone after that until she went to London Bible College. In the first fortnight she was asked out by seven different men, and knew each one of them was wrong! Then Clive came along, whom everyone else felt she should not go out with, but she just knew it was right! Ruth and Clive were married in 1973, then after two weeks of marriage Clive said he felt they should have a team, rather than his being in solo evangelism.

Ruth was angry about that. Having just got married and being trained as a teacher, she now wanted a career, but knew that if she was not on this team it would mean tremendous separation from Clive. Ruth had been holding out against the Lord over charismatic things at this time and so said, "Right Lord, whatever the outcome of this is, humanly speaking, I don't want either!" So again she threw herself on the Lord and knew then an incredible burning sweeping through her and the Lord saying, "This is the path I have chosen for you."

Clive worked as National Director of British Youth For Christ and then for Mission England. He then moved to the Evangelical Alliance. Ruth did not cope well with that because her father had been General Secretary of EA, when she was a child. So again she had to lay it all before the Lord. Ruth and Clive have written a book on the potential of a Christian marriage in God's hands, called *Growing Together*. It shares honestly the frustrations and joys of their early life together.

PAT COOK

Pat is now the executive director of the Central Asian Mission. She was born in Nuneaton near Coventry and was educated in England and in Germany. She decided to train as a nurse and midwife, and it was in training that she became a committed Christian, in the early 1960s. She then attended Bible College in Wales, where she trained for the mission field. For the last twenty-eight years, she has been in missionary work in Asia and England.

She joined CAM and went to Nepal, where she opened a leprosarium. Three years in Nepal were followed by eight years in Central West Asia. Pat also opened a small mobile clinic in the foothills of the Himalayas. After this she returned home, and has since then been commuting between West Asia and the United Kingdom.

Eight years ago she became one of the first female executive directors of a missionary society. As head of CAM, she has become involved in various councils and in visiting lonely believers in West Asia. She has a nationwide ministry and speaks regularly, challenging people here on the whole subject of world mission and the ministry of women in the Church.

JILL DANN

Jill grew up in Solihull. It was through a girls' Bible class that she became a Christian. Although she cannot put a date on this, she remembers that on one occasion in her mid-teens, when asked to give her testimony, she found she had something to say, because she knew what Jesus had done for her. She then went first to Birmingham University, and then on to Oxford to do a second degree, before being called to the Bar. At university, she was the only girl amongst forty men reading law!

Later she married Tony, who was also a lawyer, and they moved to Chippenham in Wiltshire. They then lived in the same house for thirty-three years. They have four grown-up children and had another child who died. When the children were small there were not many professional women around, so Jill was in considerable demand, speaking a lot and giving testimonies in various missions. They worked in the local church, leading Covenanters and youth work. Jill was then very home-based, but still able to see people become Christians. When the twins were still small, Tony and Jill together became Mayor and Mayoress.

Before the twins started school, an invitation came for her husband to stand for the Church Assembly — the forerunner of the General Synod of the Church of England. He pushed it over the breakfast table and said, "That is for you my dear!" Jill replied, "You must be joking, the twins are not even at school!" Having asked a group of friends to pray about it, one rang back feeling that God had asked her to help with Jill's family, if she had to go to London.

Despite her youth she stood for election, was successful and God confirmed this to her as His will during that first winter. Jill's legal training helped and she was soon to be the first woman to be elected a Church Commissioner, because she had qualifications normally only found in men, at a time when they were beginning to look for women to serve. She went on to the General Advisory Council for the Independent Broadcasting Authority and served on various councils and committees, having had the sort of training to cope with piles of papers quickly!

Jill now chairs the Church of England Evangelical Council. She succeeded John Stott and was approached after a unanimous committee decision to ask her! So, after praying about it seriously, she added this to her other roles. She was also on the standing committee of the Church of England Synod, and is now its lay vice-chairman. One other job she had for ten years was to be a member of the Crown Appointments Commission which nominates to the Prime Minister two people to be Bishops in the Church, whenever a vacancy occurs. Jill has never sought any of these positions and would rather have done more things at home with her husband and in the local community. God, however, has said that her service is to be wider than just in her local community.

REVD JEAN DARNALL

Jean was born in Charleston, West Virginia. Later, on moving to Toledo, Ohio, Jean was healed of a serious deteriorating kidney disease and her family was converted as a result of her healing. In her mid-teens she was called to a preaching ministry and God has greatly blessed her, especially in the area of praying for the sick.

Later still she met Elmer at Bible College. They were married and have had two children. Elmer and Jean were missionaries in Panama and Australasia before finally coming to England in 1966, where they have remained in response to a vision that God gave. Here Jean has been involved with 'Festival of Light', 'Come Together', and 'If My People' presentations. Part of the vision that God gave showed fires of spiritual awakening flowing from Scotland down over the British Isles.

Jean believes now that the purpose of the present renewal is to prepare the Church for an awakening that will change Britain, with multitudes converted and many sent out as witnesses to Europe. She has recently felt a definite call to Scotland. Jean has written the story of how God has led her in *Heaven Here I Come!* and *Life In The Overlap*. She and Elmer with their children have also written a daily devotional book called *Faith For The Family*.

VALERIE GRIFFITHS

Valerie has been a Christian since the age of eleven. Her family attended an Open Brethren assembly. She went through the usual time of doubt at about sixteen, wondering if it was her parents' faith or her own. The Lord met her then and confirmed His existence to her. For a number of years in her early teens she planned to study nursing, but gradually the Lord began pointing her towards RE teaching. After doing the old school certificate she switched from Science to Arts. Her school went to great lengths to enable her to take RE at A level, with the necessary Latin and Greek. When she left school, she helped at the EMMS Hospital in Nazareth for four months in 1952, when the state of Israel was struggling to establish itself.

It was there that she began to hear the Lord calling her overseas. Nazareth is an Arab town, with both Muslims and Christians, and many of the women coming in and out daily were illiterate. She realised as never before that unless someone shared the Christian message with them, millions would never hear it, because they could not read. She returned to Britain to study theology at college, rather reluctantly. Study seemed a waste of time compared with the life and death situation she had left. Later she realised how little use she would have been anywhere at that stage.

At college she met Mike, who had already graduated and was doing an ordination course and praying about Africa. Her heart was still in Israel! Gradually South-East Asia emerged for them as a forgotten area with a population a little smaller than Africa, but greater than all of Latin America. Six months after marriage, they applied to the Overseas Missionary Fellowship and sailed for the Far East in 1957. After four months in Singapore at OMF International Headquarters, they sailed on to Japan, with a four-week-old son. The first four years there were spent laying foundations, doing two years of full-time language study and evangelism, plus work with new churches.

OMF later seconded Mike to the Kirisutosha Gakuseikai (UCCF) in Tokyo at their request. Ten years later Mike was asked to move to OMF headquarters in Singapore. They were there for thirteen years until 1980, when they returned to England to the London Bible College. During those years in Singapore, Mike was away up to five months each year, visiting missionaries. Valerie saw the ladies' meetings develop, eventually into the Japanese Christian Fellowship, when they were able to call their own pastor from Japan. In Singapore she also picked up theology again when the Discipleship Training Centre needed help with the London Diploma of Theology. By that time they had four children, the first and last born in Singapore, the middle two in Japan. Valerie has become well-known for her writing since her return from the Far East. She has lectured to students at the London Bible College, when her husband was the principal, but is at present with him in Canada.

PATRICIA HIGTON

Patricia became a Christian at seven. Her father was an Anglican vicar. She remembers at the age of twelve a very definite call to full-time service. At that time God gave her a vision of the second coming, which made such an impact on her that she was able to say to Him that she would serve Him in whatever way He wanted. She felt then it would probably mean medical work of some description, but at seventeen she saw the need in schools to have teachers of religious education who were believers. To do this she needed theological training and eventually went to London Bible College.

At Bible College she met Tony, and it was in 1967, while a student, that she was baptised in the Spirit. Patricia then taught while Tony trained for the Anglican ministry. She has now been married to Tony for twenty-five years and they have two children, a daughter who is a student nurse and a son who is eighteen. They moved in 1975 to their parish in Essex after Tony had worked in two curacies.

Both Patricia and Tony have become better known since founding ABWON, Action for Biblical Witness to Our Nation. At the time when this was started, Tony was also voted onto the General Synod of the Church of England. Alongside their home commitments, they are consultants to over 40 churches in the UK and an increasing number abroad, mostly of traditional background, whose ministers are involved in renewal and looking for a return to New Testament principles. Patricia's ministry is prophetic and one of encouragement and challenge.

SALLY McCLUNG

Sally was born in Galveston in Texas, the youngest in a family of nine. As a baby her mother dedicated her to missionary service. When she was five years old, she knew God was calling her to a life of mission. As a teenager, Sally grew up in the church and taught in Sunday School, amongst other things. At this time, a feeling came that there had to be more to the Christian life and she went through a year of personal turmoil. She then became acquainted with Youth With A Mission and met her future husband Floyd at her first YWAM outreach in Las Vegas, Nevada.

Sally then participated in a summer outreach to the Samoan Islands when she was sixteen years old. Following high school graduation she went to work as a secretary in the YWAM office in Pasadena, California. Two and a half years after they met and the day after Floyd graduated from Southern California College, Floyd and Sally were married on June 2, 1967. They now have two teenage children, Misha and Matthew.

Three days after getting married they left to lead 75 young people on a summer of service in the Caribbean. It was four years before they finally unpacked their suitcases and settled down! Their early involvement in YWAM took them on a missionary trip around the world. It was then that God spoke to them about the needs of the young people from the West travelling along the hippie trail. They returned to Kabul, Afghanistan and there Dilaram Houses were birthed. These houses were healing communities to young people on the fringes of society. Sally and Floyd opened their home and hearts to 'world travellers' on the hippie trail. Many of these young people were destitute, sick and homeless. Their story is told in the book *Living On The Devil's Doorstep*.

In 1973, Sally moved with Floyd to Amsterdam with a burden for the people in the city. Urban Missions, a ministry to prostitutes, drug addicts and street people grew from that burden. Floyd has become Executive Director of International Operations for YWAM. As this ministry has grown, so has their involvement with the Body of Christ in Holland. Sally is a member of the Amsterdam Council and speaks throughout the nation and greater Europe. She also shares from her missionary experiences on victorious Christian living. She teaches, counsels and writes. Some of her articles have been published in both English and Dutch periodicals. She has recently written her first book, called *Where Will I Find The Time?* Sally has a special heart for women in leadership and for the ministry of biblical hospitality.

CHRISTINE NOBLE

Christine is an East London girl and some of her earliest memories are of bombs being dropped during the Battle of Britain. Her family was matriarchal and of Jewish descent. Her religious background was full of spiritism and also contained a strong desire for the supernatural. Most of her childhood was spent in Ilford and here she developed a talent for acting and went to the Royal Academy. During her time there she met her future husband John.

The 'hole inside that only God can fill' was there when she was young, and at sixteen she wanted to become a Roman Catholic, but a year later finally decided on the Anglican Church. At about the time she met John, then a worldly young man and a backslidden Christian, she began 'shopping', going from church to church. The 'hole inside', however, did not go away, and together they began to seek the supernatural. Seances did not satisfy and they returned to the Anglican Church, which John also joined.

Neither of them were real Christians at this point and when they were married, they went on 'hunting for God'. They tried all the denominations and finally met up with a real Christian couple who believed in the Bible. This resulted in nightly readings of the New Testament, rather like a novel! Later the same couple began to share with them about their experience of God. As a result, John came back to God and Christine decided to give God a whirl! The dance has been going on ever since!

They were both filled with the Spirit and started a new way of life. This included the demonstration of God's power, which for them meant that their needs were met, money multiplied and people were set free to serve the Lord. Soon they were involved in establishing a fellowship in Romford, where God could be as much at home as the people in the fellowship. Out from that home base Christine's ministry has opened up. She has herself written a book called *What in the World is God Saying about Women?*, expressing her own radical feelings on the whole issue of womanhood in and out of the Church today.

BREN ROBSON

Bren was born in the north of England in an isolated farming community. She was in a man's world, but she was a girl and as such continuously felt that she was a mistake! Her childhood was traumatic. Her parents were not believers, and she was nine when she first met Jesus. She remembers in her early childhood preaching to her mother. Having had the surgical removal of one eye when one and a half years old, as a child she prayed that she would have two eyes. When Jesus did not replace it she gave up trying and lost hope until her early twenties.

Bren attended a senior school in the south-east of England, having chosen to leave home. Culture shock followed for about a year. She felt lost, alone and without identity. College in London followed this, where she trained to teach, and her career began near Guildford. She began attending David Pawson's church, and when he spoke she knew that he had the life that she had really been searching for.

She has been in leadership in one way or another since 1972. First in youth work, then in developing a new children's work and also in heading up an Arts Festival, and producing a musical drama called *Children of the King*. From 1976 a woman called Mary Jones was used by God to help reshape Bren's character and life. In 1981 she felt God call her to share the lead in a fresh work and establish a new church. That is not to say that the church she left is not valid, but God wanted something quite new in the town.

So Guildford Community Church was born, where Phil Vogel, Terry Brewer and Bren were in leadership. Phil and Terry had then to decide whether Bren was there by default or design! At a leaders' conference when Ian Andrews had been giving words around the room, he looked straight at Bren and said, "You do not need deliverance, you need to know that you are anointed and called by God." It was from that time that she began to feel comfortable in building the church. The work has now developed into two congregations, both of which Bren leads.

Bren was then given a public leadership place, responsibility and opportunity to fulfil every function of leadership that a man would do. She also began to speak and teach in meetings, lead worship and has set up the whole pastoral structure of the church, but perhaps has had most influence in terms of the management side of the work, developing leaders and ministries. Six years ago she joined John Noble's Team Spirit, and is now involved in an executive role in Dave Tomlinson's Team Work. She has written a book on women in leadership called *The Turning Tide*.

PAT TOMLINSON

Pat is the administrator of Team Work, which her husband Dave began in 1982. She became involved in 1983, and has been constantly aware of God moving her on in the work of heading up the administration. She is also actively involved in the inner city fellowship in Brixton that she and Dave felt God call them to in the early 1980s.

Born in Derbyshire of Christian parents, Pat attended the nearest church to their home which happened to be Congregational. At eighteen, she went to training college in Ripon, Yorkshire. She had learned a lot in her church upbringing and was into drama, speaking in the meetings and taking responsibility. She had no hang-ups about women taking part in church life at any level.

At college she met Dave, entered into a personal experience of the Lord for herself and was baptised in the Spirit. She joined a house-group linked to a Bible teacher. This, plus the fact that Dave has a Brethren background, resulted in the whole feeling of what she could be and do as a woman in the church becoming totally different. There was a restriction on women, and also an emphasis on 'dying' to everything that one needed to 'die to' in those days! This was quite a hard time for Pat.

Marriage came after college and living in Liverpool was a

fairly low-key time. Three children, Jenny, Paul and Lizzy, came early on in marriage, followed by another move to Ripon to start a House Church fellowship. Dave felt that looking after the children and home was Pat's lot in those days, and on Sundays the whole fellowship came to a meal after the meeting. Pat's weekend was spent shopping on Saturday for the food and preparing it, then Sunday was spent at the meeting, serving the lunch and clearing up. Pat says that they have come a long way since then!

After eight years in Ripon, they went to Middlesbrough to establish the fellowship there. In 1983 Dave started the 'Festival' conferences and in 1982 Team Work was born. As a result of various problems, Pat stepped in to take over the administration of Team Work in 1983. Her children were well into secondary school, and as she enjoys administration, she got her feet under the table. Three years later Pat and Dave moved again. Dave had been thinking and preaching about Christians not abandoning the inner cities. God turned this round on him and challenged him about moving into the inner city of London. Pat now works in the office of Team Work, which is in the centre of Brixton.

DR ANNE TOWNSEND

Anne is a doctor who worked as a medical missionary in Thailand for sixteen years with her husband John, a surgeon. They have three grown-up children. She came home eight years ago to make a home for her teenage children, became full-time editor of *Family* magazine and stopped practising as a doctor. Later she was invited to become full-time director of Care Trust, with the responsibility for setting up a nationwide network of Christian families who could care for and take in people with different kinds of needs.

Anne did this for just over a year, and then had quite a severe depressive illness. Her doctor signed her off work initially for two months, but this was extended. It soon became obvious that it would be foolish for her to go back to Care Trust, because exactly the same thing could happen again. So sadly, for medical reasons, she had to stop doing that kind of work full-time. It has taken two years for Anne to get back on her feet again.

Anne also writes for the religious press. She is an Anglican and became a Christian at the age of fourteen. At confirmation she thought nothing happened when the Bishop laid his hand on her head. This she found devastating. She then asked God, that if it was possible for her to know Him, He would somehow break through to her. This He did that summer at a Youth For Christ rally, while she was on holiday.

Later on Anne sensed God clearly saying that she should marry John, and that they should become missionaries. Another breakthrough for her came in her early days of being a Christian writer. God spoke clearly about the need for total honesty in her writing, otherwise she felt the gift could not be used as God intended it to be. Such honesty was costly for a missionary who was expected to present a certain image!

God called her to write as opposed to specialising in medicine, and this has included a series of books under the title *Without Pretending*. There were books with that title on Prayer (*Prayer Without Pretending*), Marriage, Families, Missionary, and Suffering. She wrote two books for parents, one for parents of teenagers and one for single parents. She then wrote a children's book about how the body works, which has gone into about fourteen languages so far. Anne feels that God has called her to fill gaps where no one else is writing on a subject. She is at present training for ordination in the Anglican Church.

ANITA TRAYNAR

Anita was born in Bristol and moved when she was five years old to near Manchester. She went to a very lively evangelical Anglican church, and was converted under the ministry of Dick Rees. At fifteen she moved back to Bristol, which she found very difficult, because she could not find the equivalent Anglican church in the Bristol area. Her spiritual life was going into the city for British Youth For Christ rallies, once a month.

When she was in the sixth form a boy called Eric, the brother of Pete Lyne, started to talk one day about the Lord. His family had just come out of the Baptist Church and started a house fellowship. She started going along until she went to college. Anita was at Dartford PE College for four years. In the third year she met John and Christine Noble. When she moved to the Essex area to teach in 1970, she lived with them. In 1971 she met Ian, who also lived with John and Chris, and they were married in 1972. They have had four children, one of whom, Nikola, died in her cot in 1977.

Living in Collier Row, Romford she helped Christine Noble establish a playgroup. The elders then asked her to research the start of a school. She was answerable to them in the area of vision, although her friend Marion worked it through practically. She was also asked to become an administrator for a group of men who were meeting together locally. Out of this 'Team Spirit' was born.

She became part of the local fellowship leadership team, and remained there for about one and a half years. She is now on an Evangelical Alliance Coalition for education and a committee working with people in South Africa. She is also involved in school work with Christians In Education with the trustees Lyndon Bowring, Michael Fenton-Jones, Lynn Murdock and Michael Hastings, and is their consultant on Christian schools. Anita has had a prophecy that God was going to use her in education in Britain and abroad. Although she finds her work in education is not as immediately fulfilling as administration, she does feel that God has called her to this field. Anita is soon to start writing on her vision and work with Christians in education.

EILEEN VINCENT

Eileen and Alan were married in 1953, but it was not until 1958 that they were both converted. As they were encouraged to read the Bible, God was able to break into their lives. Within days they were leading people to the Lord and speaking from platforms. After her conversion Eileen was turned upside down, and within months, the Lord had called her and her husband to missionary service. They left for India in February 1963, without a mission sending them, because Alan was so ill. They went by faith, trusted God and learned an incredible amount.

Alan had a condition where he bled profusely from his nose — pints of blood at a time. He used to have blood transfusions to keep him alive. He had had every known treatment, but nothing helped. His lung collapsed and he was immobilised through asthma. He was skin and bone, with no energy to walk up stairs or digest his food, and was incredibly anaemic. This affected every area of their lives as he even bled in bed, driving the car, preaching or whatever. Eileen was always washing bloodstained clothing. She did anything that was physically hard or heavy, and had to be the strong 'man' around the place. Everyone felt they should stay at home, but they felt the Lord was telling them to go.

They continued to live by faith and were baptised in the Spirit in 1965 in Bombay. The experience transformed their ministry in the Baptist Church, where they worshipped. They had gone to the Gospel Literature Service, a Brethren work, Alan being appointed as a printing technician, but they did not feel able to worship with them, as they were Baptists back home. They lived in India for ten years with a three-year gap in the middle.

Eileen had a two-and-a-half-year-old child when they first went out, and was twenty-nine weeks pregnant with another one, which was practically born on the boat! She was in labour on the boat, not a happy state as she had lost her first child four days after birth, which did not help her mentally. They arrived with nowhere to live and Alan ill. Besides church planting in Bombay, they had a very wide ministry to many missionaries across India, and spoke at conventions. When their third child was born Eileen started writing, initially their own story, as since arriving in India she had written extended prayer letters like 'Vistas of India', and so she continued to write.

In 1972, in the middle of an incredible outpouring of the Spirit in Bombay, thousands were saved and baptised in the Spirit. During that time the great need was for teaching materials. So they began to produce a magazine called *Outpouring Magazine*. They organised a group called Trinity Fellowship in order to teach the new converts. Eileen edited the magazine. Coming home in 1976, they needed family life, and the children needed secondary education. They knew that they had come to the end of what they were doing. They returned to a church they had founded here during the three years they were home from India, between 1966 and 1969. Eileen continues her writing and has completed a new book about C. T. Studd.

MARION WHITE

Marion lives with her husband Rob at Cleobury, at the headquarters of British Youth for Christ. Having been raised in a Christian family, she made her own commitment to the Lord at fourteen years of age. She and Rob married twenty years ago and lived first in Sussex. Being a trained infant teacher, she found herself involved in church youth work with Rob.

After six years of marriage she was baptised in the Spirit. Then twins were born into the family, both girls. Jo and Debbie are now seventeen and Naomi is four years younger. It was out of the youth work that they felt called into full-time ministry, which they called 'Open House'. They knew the Lord wanted to use their home and wanted them to take people in. It was not Rob being called and Marion trailing along behind, but a definite call to each of them individually, at the same time. They then lived by faith for six years, in a large house with an extended family.

It was out of this work that Rob moved into Youth For Christ. A few people had told him that his ministry should go wider, after he had helped to form a fellowship in Crawley which is still going today. Within two years he took over from Clive Calver as National Director of BYFC. They moved to Cleobury just over three years ago. Again God spoke to Marion and Rob about the move and they held on to the vision for a year until they were finally able to move into the present building. Marion and Rob have written a book on practical encouragement for parents with home and church responsibilities called *My Family, My Church*.

SECTION 1

WHO DOES WHAT
OR
'CALCULATEDLY FEMALE'?

One

Identity and Function

Identity is the individual existence of a unique and valuable personality. We all need to know, woman or man, who we are. *Function*, however, is our performance and activity, which fulfils a purpose or expected action. This, for most of us, is the factor on which our value depends. Roger Davin, a Bible teacher from Duluth in the USA, speaking some years ago at a Christian conference, coined the phrase that 'identity precedes function'. In other words, we first must know who we are and be at peace with ourselves, in our place in the Body of Christ, before we can function in the way that God intended. Our worth and esteem must come from being recipients of God's unconditional love.

Without knowing His love, we strive on a never-ending merry-go-round of introspection, or we for ever work to project an outer image that is as acceptable as possible, both to us and to those around us. So when function precedes identity, we are gaining our acceptance and proving ourselves by *doing* endless things, rather than just by *being* ourselves. This brings pressure into life, as we move into living under law, rather than living under the grace of God. For centuries, countless women and men in and out of the Church have lived on a functional basis, doing the things that have been expected of them.

History, culture and tradition have aimed death blows at womanhood. We find male chauvinism right back in the ancient world, where the Greeks often thought of women as lying somewhere between animals and deformed men. Women were on the same level as slaves, under the authority and control of their husbands, by custom and law. Although Plato believed in the equality of the sexes, which was an unusual view, Aristotle held the more normal view that women were the inferior sex.

A good Jew might pray and thank God that he was not created a Gentile, a slave or a woman! He was also encouraged not to talk too much with women, for fear of bringing evil upon himself! Jews shared the universal concept of the inferiority of women, but unlike Muslims, did not sanction total subjection of women to men. However, a female child was not rejoiced over as much as a boy, and the rabbi did not give her the same instruction as a male child. The law was not considered something a female mind could grasp!

That men were more important than women was enshrined in Jewish law. A man could easily divorce his wife; a woman had to ask permission of her husband first! Her financial value was often considered less than that of an animal bought in the marketplace. So women were not people in their own right, rather things to be possessed, with no legal rights at all. Is it any wonder that women have risen up against such a history and against such attitudes in the more recent past?

God, however, had something else in mind from the beginning. He created man, male and female after His own image (Genesis 1:27). The word 'man' is more correctly translated as 'mankind' or 'humankind', rather than male man. God Himself within His image has both male and female attributes. He is known in Isaiah 49:14-15 as mother, in Isaiah 63:16 as father and in Isaiah 66:13 again God is spoken of as a mother. In Genesis 17:1, we have the first revelation of God as El-Shaddai to Abraham. The name means Almighty and All-Sufficient One, and has the word *shad* at its root, which means female breast. These are just some of the female words for God, often forgotten when we think of God as Father only.

So God created 'mankind' in His image, to have dominion over all the earth. This 'mankind' is obviously 'male with female' in relationship. They were to share life together. Neither is considered any differently from the other as far as foundational identity is concerned. They may function differently, but Eve is bone of Adam's bone, and flesh of Adam's flesh, being formed from the same substance as the man, and being made in the image of the same God. Adam and Eve together are God's created 'mankind'.

As a result of sin, changes come into creation. God says that the husband will tend to rule over the woman, because her desire will be for him first, rather than for God. So, as far as identity is concerned, the fall makes Adam dominant. Dominion becomes male domination and subsequently the woman shrinks to become inferior. We see this worked out straightaway in their replies to God. Adam strongly blames the woman for his sin, and indirectly blames God who gave him the woman. Eve in weakness admits she has been deceived and puts herself down.

In the Old Testament we find some women able and secure enough to share some areas of life with the men. A few owned land, some were very enterprising. One was a well-known judge, Deborah; one was a queen, Esther, who altered the course of history. Tradition, however, crept into Jewish life. We see a gradual decline in the woman's role, identity and place, with such developments as a woman's testimony not being acceptable in a court of law.

Jesus broke into this scene, to break the curse of the fall for women. His attitude was that of a radical revolutionary. He saw women as personalities in their own right. It was He who, when it was forbidden to talk to women by tradition, communicated with them publicly, even with a low prostitute. He, who had been taught the attitude that it was better to burn the words of the law than to teach it to a woman, allowed Mary to sit at His feet in the discipleship position! She, He said, had chosen the better part, and was in the learning phase of her life. What fruit she must have borne!

Jesus was a man who had feminine qualities too. He was not afraid to let it be known that He was not 'macho'. He saw the needs of people around Him, as a mother does, and understood when they lacked food or rest. He was able to cook a breakfast and willing to wash dirty feet. He loved having the children around and was not afraid to cuddle them. He organised men to give food out to people and serve, and to clean up afterwards! He said in Luke 13:34, "Oh Jerusalem ... how often I have longed to gather your children together, as a hen gathers her chicks under her wings", and you cannot be more feminine in attitude than that!

Later in the New Testament, in Romans 16 Paul lists women who have laboured in the gospel with him. These women had identity and function and were very liberated, working alongside the men in the early Church. Restrictions, however, began to be placed back on women as time went on, as we shall see later.

But what is God saying to the Church at the end of the twentieth century? Are women people in their own right, with their own identity? And if that is true, can they have a personal ministry and function in the Church? Are there common thoughts and feelings amongst well-known women in leadership in the Church today?

The first thing that I became aware of in talking to this group of women was that they all knew that they had a special relationship with God. They knew they were unique and that their lives, though not without their struggles, had a purpose.

Christine Noble, for example, says, "Yes, I'm a unique creation in God. It is the snowflake principle; everyone is unique. The counterfeiter turns out things that are the same, greed, avarice, hate, etc. But in Psalm 139, the Bible says that we are each fashioned in the womb, a one-off, and then the mould is broken. In God's economy, if I do not fill the place that He has earmarked for me, in His kingdom, then He's missing me. Not that He could not work it out without me, but He would still miss me if I was not there."

The theme of knowing that she is special is developed by **General Eva Burrows**. "One of the wonderful things about our faith is that God is interested in every individual person. I believe God has a plan for us as individuals. This is particularly shown in the life of Christ. Although the crowds followed Him, He seemed to be happiest when He was speaking individually to people. To Him every person had worth and value.

"I see this working out in our lives too. I believe some of the situations that people call coincidences in life, are in fact incidences of God's personal concern for us. In my own life such things have happened to me many times. Once, when I had decided to stay back in Australia for a year and take a master's degree, I was a little uncertain but had taken the decision to do it, believing it was right.

"When I was sitting on the deck of the boat taking me back to Australia, the man sitting in the next chair began to talk with me. It turned out that he was the professor from Australia who had handled my papers for the university, and was he pleased to meet me! This was a real confirmation to me personally about what I was doing. Therefore, I know that God is interested in me and, as a result, I have some tasks which He wants *me* to do, rather than anyone else. This is not head knowledge, but a knowledge that I experience in life. I really have that feeling of God directing my life."

So we see that the hand of God is at work in both creating and directing unique and individual lives. Yet so often many of us do not know that this is our birthright and we fail to develop our potential in God. For many women the struggle starts with real acceptance of their being female.

Anita Traynar is very honest as she shares concerning her gender. "Ever since I've been saved, I have always felt that I am a person in my own right before God. In the early days, the problem I did have, however, within the House Church as it was then in our stream, was the strong male orientation. I can remember going to college and being very cross with God, wanting to do so much for Him and yet I felt blocked because I was not male. I can remember being angry that He had made me female, and therefore second-class. I was asking constantly if anything I did for God would count in the same way as the things that men did.

"After getting through this anger, I heard God saying to me that He just wanted me to serve. In that way I would serve people around me, which would be serving Him, and so I would grow. I embraced this, particularly when I got involved with John and Christine Noble. Then slowly, because John never had a problem with women moving in their own realm of gift, I felt built up again, whereas I had been quite heavily knocked in the early years.

"So I knew there was a calling of God on my life that I was able to walk in. It was not a mistake that I was female, and I began to walk more clearly. There are still a lot of pockets of male dominance in the House Churches, which I meet more now that I am out on the education circuit, moving across the streams. You feel certain streams embrace you, because of your gifting and the work that you have done, regardless of the fact that you are a woman, but others are still extremely suspicious. They then grapple with their relationship with you, because what they are being taught is different from what they are actually working with in reality. It is not so much that women are second-class, as that they seem to be treated as though they are of a different stature from the men."

So we women have often had to deal with feeling inferior and fearful. This can lead to depression, despair, anger and rebellion. Women are rising up in an attempt to overcome, yet even that very attempt can lead up a blind alley. As **Sue Barnett** says, "We hear a lot about rights in this day and age. Whenever we talk about grasping things for ourselves, it implies that we are not fulfilled. But I have found in knowing Jesus I am very fulfilled and I don't have to grasp for what God has already given me. Not only am I a special child of His, but He gives me a special job to do. Being trained in college for three years has developed my ministry of teaching, and was ideal preparation for my present work in encouraging and equipping Christians and communicating the gospel."

Women were never intended by God to be set against men, just as they are not to be 'put down'. "God made each of us, men and women, to be a part of His creation and glorify Him. The completeness of the male and female is together in unity," says **Sylvia Mary Alison**. "Yet each part is infinitely precious and worthwhile. Jesus loves each one of us so much. He poured out His life for me, and therefore I would do myself and Him a great disservice by running myself down. I am of infinite worth to Him, and therefore I must be careful not to do myself damage. I feel each one of us is called as part of the body of Christ to minister to one another and build one another up. Our gifts are not to be selfishly hoarded but used for the common good.''

Sally McClung believes that God made women because they were needed. She explains, ''If we were exactly like men, we would not have needed to be custom-made. We are different but more than just biologically. This does not mean that we are weak. There is strength in our fibre. When our husbands or other men fall apart, often they rely on us or women around them. The Lord has built into us a softness, a gentleness, a sensitivity and a great capacity for love. I believe He wants to use these things. We have a capacity to minister, to comfort, to heal, to build up and to encourage. It is important to keep those areas and dimensions as part of us, especially as and when we move into leadership.

''I often say when I am teaching that we have seasons in our lives, and sometimes we try to rush them. We wish it was summer, when it is still winter. It is very important to accept the season we are now in and allow God to bring about the release for that, rather than for future seasons. In Philippians we are told to be content in all circumstances. For us, as women, that is important. As God is releasing us into what He has for us now, we need to be content where we are, rather than try and push something ahead of its time. We need to be careful that we don't wish for the past and long for the future! We need to work and allow God to lead us into the next step, and enjoy the different seasons of our lives.''

The ultimate need a woman has for identity and the clashes that this can sometimes produce is highlighted for us by **Marion White**. She shares how for her, an identity 'crisis' came and was resolved within her marriage. ''I think that the most exciting thing about being a Christian is that God loves us as individuals. I do believe I can have a personal ministry. However, I used to be exceedingly shy, always very happy to let Rob take the lead. I did not want to be in the limelight, rather in the shadows. In fact, I realise now that I just leaned on him spiritually, without really developing my own life.

"We clashed a lot in our early marriage, because he came from a Brethren background, where the women wore hats and did not take part. It was an accepted part of life. The thing that affected me most was when he would ask me if I had had my quiet time, or if I had done this or that. I felt he was patronising me, so I just rebelled and said that if he was going to push me, I wasn't going to do anything! So I stagnated.

"It was not until we were filled with the Spirit that Rob himself saw me as a person in my own right. It was then that with his help and encouragement I began to have a real liberating sense of all that this means. I was a woman, who was God's child and could equally share the gifts and abilities He had given me. Being shy, I did not want to do anything publicly. Yet as God led us on, we had so much to share, particularly in Open House. There we had seen the grace of God in our lives, while living by faith. So I started in a small way speaking about it, and because we had a small growing fellowship, I began to take part in that and lead other women who were younger than me. I saw the need, and the more I realised what I had in God the more excited I became, which gave me added confidence to continue."

So a major key in our search for identity is our openness to the Holy Spirit. If God is calling us, He will enable and train us. **Valerie Griffiths** echoes this from her experience. "I believe God called me to full-time Christian service and gave me the spiritual training I needed to serve Him. Overseas where Christians were few, I responded freely to whatever situation I faced, as best I could, whether evangelistic, pastoral, teaching, administration, etc.

"I find it extraordinary here in Britain that the service of women is so confined by unbiblical traditions, assumptions, expectations and prejudices which prevent them from fulfilling God's call and enabling power. It is time Christians stopped arguing over what women may not do, and instead made a realistic evaluation of how they should be using the gifts the Holy Spirit has given them. We need to ask how we as women fulfil our calling as priests to God as stated in Revelation 1:5-6.

"The word of God is both the basis and authority for any teaching we give, and this is true for any Christian man or woman. My call to full-time service has been recognised by my church and fellow Christians according to the Scriptural requirement in 1 Thessalonians 5:19-21. It would therefore be disobedient for me to back out and be silent.

"This prior call to service has been fulfilled in the context of home, marriage, husband and children, but it has never been cancelled by these other responsibilities. Both husband and wife in Christian work need to recognise that they are called together and separately, and both must work out what this means in enabling the other partner to fulfil God's calling to them. The nature of service overseas makes it essential that each is called personally to such work. It ought to be considered equally important for service in this country too.

"This was underlined for us when we joined OMF in 1957, and has set the pattern for our marriage ever since. We were interviewed individually, and both received the same financial support. I was treated as a person in my own right, with my family commitments as a wife and mother. I was expected to learn the language and be involved in evangelism and teaching."

Myra Blyth also believes that every person has a ministry, linked to their unique personality. "In terms of the priesthood of all believers, we are all called and all have a vocation. That vocation is determined by the very character that God has given to each of us. I never at any point felt I did not have a vocation of some description. The fact that it has now expressed itself in a full-time ministry is almost incidental to my belief that ministry is something unique to everybody. Nobody has a self-appointed vocation! It is confirmed by others who know them best, and who can enable them to practise that gift. I never for one moment imagined that my ministry would be questioned other than on the grounds of whether the skill, talent and gift was there. Ministry should not be measured on gender. It must also be rooted in a context.

Finally, **Pat Tomlinson** underlines again for us God's work in our lives. "In today's climate, a woman's ability to take part is developing alongside how much place she is given to take part. My ministry is still developing and I have recently been asked to lead worship in meetings. I have said that I will be trained to do it, rather than just stand up and do it, because I don't feel that is fair. Men have had training and help in this. I am not saying 'no' to it, because I want to have a go! I may not be any good at leading worship, but I will try it, like a man would, and find out whether I am good in that area or not!

"I feel it is abysmal that the preacher is thought of more highly than the one who cleans the toilets. It is my lifelong ambition to see this brought into balance. If I am the one who cleans the toilet, then I am happy to be that one. That is partly the reason I carry on in administration, because it is not given a very high appreciation profile and I want to help see that redressed."

The consensus of feeling amongst these women in leadership is very clear. All women are created in the image of God, just as men are, and as such have gifts and abilities which must be utilised and allowed to function within the context of the Church. Having taken time to find out who we are in God, with the necessary healing that many of us need in our souls, and counsel as to what He wants each one of us to do, we then have the only secure foundation on which to build our lives and ministry.

Jesus is our pattern. When He was baptised, John the Baptist said, "Behold the Lamb of God." This was His identity in a nutshell. Then followed these words, "who takes away the sin of the world." This was His primary function. However, God said of Him, "This is My beloved Son, in whom I am well pleased," and these words were spoken before Jesus had done any ministry, works or wonders. Jesus was secure first in knowing He was loved and knowing who He was. Then He moved out in ministry. We too need to hear how much God loves and accepts us, before we do anything for Him.

We have our identity in Christ. Being a new creation takes time to get used to! We become secure if we know we are made and loved by God, as we are, male or female, each one unique. We are, in fact, so valuable to Him that He was prepared to come and die to redeem us from slavery, to place us back into His family, giving us a purpose and a future. As Ephesians 2:10 says, ''We are God's workmanship, created in Christ Jesus to do good works, which God prepared in advance for us to do.''

Eve's and Adam's identity was in being like God, in both His being and doing. We have an awareness of being an 'I am'. We also have an awareness of having work to do, of a need to take action rather than move in reaction to things in life. It is only God who can give us back our true identity and function, which has been marred by sin. He loves us, forgives us, accepts us just as we are and heals us. We are, each one, a person He has created and with whom He wants a personal relationship, for ever.

Most women have not fully known that they have been made in the image of God. They have not understood that at the root of their being God made them 'calculatedly' female. They are, therefore, unique, valuable and of eternal worth, whatever the world around them says to the contrary. So many have been identity-hungry, continually dissatisfied, having a negative feeling about themselves. They have often tried to establish who they are through manipulation, self-assertion and self-pity. Many have been damaged and have false identities, where parts of their personalities are passive or repressed and need God's healing touch.

Once women know before God that they are not second-class, but are each unique, created in God's image and in relationship with a loving God, who accepts them personally, then they are at peace. Even if they never do anything for Him, they know His acceptance of them is total. From this secure base, being given a place in the Body of Christ, they are then able to begin to function as their gifts and abilities develop. Women can function in all the gifts of the Holy Spirit. It is abilities and callings, not male and female, which is the issue.

At different seasons in their lives, women can follow the leadings of the Holy Spirit. They have a developing sense of becoming and being an 'I am', a person who is a reflection of the Creator. This must precede any role or function. Basic security in life starts here. Then the Church, including husbands and male leaders, needs to affirm and encourage and facilitate, as women begin to understand that their heritage is also to have dominion over some part of the world to some degree.

The myth that Eve is a secondary or subservient creation (because Adam was created first and Eve second) needs to be firmly knocked on the head. When God created Adam, Adam alone was good yet incomplete. So Eve was made as a companion for Adam. Adam called her *Ishah*, which means she-man, and in Hebrew sounds like the word for man. She was the very last of God's creation, and, dare we say it, the very best? Adam thought so! At last he had found 'she' whom his soul would love. He had a partner equal to himself with whom he could enjoy living in the garden of Eden. It has been said of old that if man is the head, woman is the crown, a crown to her husband, the crown of visible creation. God often seems to keep the best wine until last. If we have something of the essence of this attitude about our female identity, we will be able to begin to walk humbly along the path I believe Jesus wants to walk along with us, as women of God, side by side with men of God.

Two

Feminism

The feminist movement has grown up in our recent past in response to what feminists feel is the total lack of recognition of women and their lack of equality of opportunity with men. Books have been written showing how some women only live their lives through their husbands and children, without knowing their own personal *identity*. Their *function* is thus seen as little more than unfulfilled sexual satisfiers and cleaning machines. Their vocation is simply said to be a support to their men. This form of 'slavery' is seen by feminists to be dehumanising, as such women are often well-educated. Often slipping into the mental fog of passive entrapment, they are said to become victims of a system which often ends in hostility, violence, or a breakdown of one kind or another.

Some feminists are more politically minded, and see traditional structures like the family, school and churches as promoting a hierarchical structure which, within capitalism, maintains the status quo. Mixed amongst these feminists are those who ask if a male deity can save women from a male-dominated system of life. They want to rewrite Scripture making God mother. They cannot relate to or countenance a father God, for whatever reason, and therefore substitute mother God into their theology. Here we have the beginnings of so-called Goddess religion.

Some radical feminists can be real men-haters and some are even found calling for the development of artificial reproduction to free women from child-bearing and what they see as subsequent slavery. Some even hope to see the day when scientists can fertilise an egg in the laboratory without male sperm, leading to the day when sperm will be unnecessary, with the possibility of an all-female world. Such women really want male exclusion!

Feminism today has brought the whole issue of women's identity out into the light, but its solution tends to be to push women towards the aggressive, competitive male-dominating identity. This is because such women feel themselves in competition with men. Many feminists also feel that identity is to be found in what a woman does or has, or what she achieves.

As we have already seen, history, culture and tradition have all played their part in this issue. We can see it from the Garden of Eden, where the battle of the sexes began and with it, for the first time, violence came into creation. Enmity was sown between the man and the woman, and there we see the beginning of conflict. Male dominance and female fear and subservience began to be worked out in the relationship.

We have already seen something of Bible history in this matter, but continuing from the early Church fathers, gradually through the years, the so-called inferiority of women to men began to be spoken about frequently. We find it in Clement's writing around 200 AD. He writes primarily of women at home and little about women in relation to the Church.

Tertullian is reported as saying around the same time that women are subjected ... throughout to men! He goes on to say that women are "the Devil's gateway, the unsealer of that tree, the first deserter of divine law ..." Also, "You (woman) destroyed so easily God's image, man. On account of your desert even the Son of God had to die."

About half a century later, Cyprian writes that women were not to speak in church and so women's ministry in the Church was further reduced. In the sixth century AD, at Mâçon in France, the council of churches debated the motion that 'women have a soul'. The motion was carried by one vote! Right through history up to today many women have been taught that their primary function is to be 'under authority'. This, say the pro-feminists, is enough reason to sound the battle cry.

Within the last two centuries we have seen Wilberforce fight to end slavery and we now abhor racism, yet it seems ironic that often we still struggle even to see the paternalistic society of male dominating female as an issue of injustice. Any form of discrimination means that some are entitled and others are not and nearly always it is the weaker who suffer.

What is the Church's reply to all this? At times it seems very muddled. Some churches believe one thing, some another. One insists that women remain silent, others that they wear head coverings. Some churches have such a male image of God that women are crippled in their fuctioning. They are reduced to a supporting role, frustrated in their ability to pastor or teach, often while a man performs these roles without any flair at all. Many churches are embarrassed to have mature women capable of being leaders. Often only overseas missionary work is open to them.

Men can so often put women down, patronising them or telling them that they must be under authority. This often has its source in male insecurity, in not knowing what to do with capable, mature women, or how to react towards them. How often has a man thought, ''Why can't a woman be more like a man?''

Christians who really are against the feminists often see them as evil, without finding out anything about what they are saying. They tend to think that all feminists are wanting to break up family life and that children are suffering as a result. They see them as promiscuous. The stereotype is set: women are to be in submission somewhere, dependent and without responsibility, and this is the kind of feminine woman that a masculine man wants.

They look on in horror at the feminist demonstrations, where the media 'home in' on the abusive incidents, but they forget or may not know how earlier feminists were sometimes godly women who have effected changes in the law which benefit all women today. Many Christians are retreating from this chaos, aiming to bring back order into the Church. The result is that they are putting women back into their place, as they see it. But as Derek Poole, a Bible teacher from Northern Ireland, so ably said, speaking at a conference on 'Women and Men Together in Leadership', ''The essence of spiritual life is tension and paradox, not neat packages. If the head wins we go off into reason, if the heart wins we drift into super-spirituality and discredit the things of the Spirit. Both must work together. Neither must win; if one wins, both lose."

Other Christians who favour the general movement of feminism tell us that we must be prominent in any pursuit of justice in relation to women. We are told that we must stand up for the rights of individuals who are being misused or abused, whatever the cost. Too many women live lives of drudgery, and too many men are fulfilled in their work, as well as in the Church. The system is not fair and so the fight is on.

So who is right and what is the consensus of opinion and belief amongst the leading women of the Church today? How do they think about feminism? What do they feel are God's desires in this matter?

Jean Darnall feels that feminism is more of a cultural problem than a spiritual one. "People not even acquainted with Christianity are usually the most strident and outspoken. In history, the suffragettes were often very godly women, in contrast to many modern feminists who are really pagan. I know some Christians who have felt that they needed to get into that movement and give it some Christian flavour, because there is a lot of injustice against women.

"If I was a woman working in the world, in an office or factory or in government, I would probably feel as strongly as some of them do about the inequalities for working women. But I cannot identify with their methods of asserting themselves, because that is so unchristian. We have laid down our rights at the cross, and whatever the Lord gives back to us, we gratefully receive and use as wisely as we can. But they are not 'my' rights, they are the privileges the Lord has given me. It is an unchristian attitude to demand rights for ourselves, but fighting for other people's rights is quite different."

Listening to the strident feminist voice can sometimes make us think at a deeper level of the hurts and denials that many women have had. We may also need to ask whether the Church, in its suppression of women through the centuries, has almost cooked its own goose. Has it in fact been a creator of problems in this regard? Because the Church has often viewed feminism as something terrible, women in the Church have at times become frightened to say too much, for fear of being aligned with it. They have ended up just making the tea or helping in Sunday School. Valuable as these things are, they are not the sum total of a woman's Christian life.

Valerie Griffiths thinks Christians have been lagging behind, while the extreme feminists are far too individualistic and selfish. "In some situations it is very difficult to say, as a wife, that you feel your husband should be at home more so that you can get out to do something else. Yet these women often have good education and training. The assumption that the man has to be set free for his work and calling by his wife, who then has no ministry of her own, is quite wrong. Christians need to rethink.

"If we really believe in the personhood of woman, it is as important for women to get out and fulfil their own ministry, not just remain trapped permanently in the home. Worked within the context of home, family and community I believe a wife has her calling from the Lord, as well as her husband. The husband should help to see that it is fulfilled. This is part of God's answer to the feminist issue, particularly within the home and family arena."

Without God women have a vacuum to fill, which can be filled by feminism. **Myra Blyth** understands that the underlying premise of feminism is that women are often unable to take their full part in work, family, society and church. She explains, "Their role has been circumscribed by the men. This I see as the challenge of feminism and I totally understand it. I see, in every area of life, the role of women being circumscribed by institutions run by men, which formulate the norms that suit them. But this must be put into a context!

"We should not be afraid of the term 'feminist theology'. It is very exciting to me, in terms of rereading the Bible from a woman's perspective and positively reading women back into history. Jesus' attitude to women in the gospels was so liberating and so creative. I would very much want to emphasise this.

"I want to see the Christian feminist analysis of the society in which we live, within the context of politics, ethics and economics, so that it cannot be dismissed as women talking about women again, but that we are actually saying there is a woman's perspective on the fallen society in which we live. This can bring a new strand of thinking to bear on how we can see the transformation of society. Women as women can bring some unique insights to bear."

Bren Robson feels that some people are fighting the wrong battles. "We each have a calling, and we need to be responsible to discover what that is. Everybody has a part to play and we need to be free to find out what that is. The feminists, I believe, are fighting the wrong battles. They are fighting for freedom, which has already been won! Those of us who are Christians are already at liberty to make our choices and fulfil our calling. If our calling is to stay at home, we should be free to stay at home. If it is to be involved in a career, we should be free to do that. We should not put pressure on one another to stay at home or to have a vocation, for we are all equally valuable in the sight of God. Liberation is not to be free from all restraint, as some seem to feel. In the Kingdom of God, we can only be given authority; we cannot take it."

For **Rosemary Andrews** there are no 'ism's in the kingdom of God. She shares, " 'Ism's usually come out of false cults, insecurity and rebellion, and usually cause confusion and division. As a result of the fall of man and subsequent erroneous teachings, the majority of women have been led from one misbelief to another.

"The feminist movement has had some good points in giving mistreated, underprivileged and abused women a voice and a fairer deal, with the opening up of some career opportunities with equal status. However, today there are many wounded and frightened women walking around, and also some who are dominating and exerting control rooted in their anger and frustration. Neither extreme is God's plan for us as women. Paul in the New Testament said, 'Let nothing be done out of strife or vain glory.'

"Often those who pursue feminism to the extreme have come on very strong, in my opinion, out of rejection and a crushed spirit. This in turn is often built into suppressed anger, which is then released against the male species. This is just as bad as a man exerting control by force. Many women (and men) have had very little good fathering, which has left them with all sorts of insecurities and voids, colouring their opinions of men in a detrimental way.

"Jesus was always fair to women, and lifted them up from the lowly positions of that day, giving them a sense of value and usefulness. He made them feel neither inferior nor superior to the men of that day, but He showed Himself as their friend, by communicating His love and humour towards them without ever making fun of them. In the midst of a strict male-dominated culture came a man who cared and touched and mused with women and they loved Him. He must have appeared so gracious and kind in comparison to the way they had been treated. In the incident of the woman who had been haemorrhaging for twelve years, Jesus did not mention her making Him unclean (according to ceremonial law) by touching Him. Rather He took pains to compliment her on her healing faith. Her inner feelings about herself were healed too."

Jesus did not grasp after equality with God. Neither should women grasp after being like men. **Eileen Vincent** says, "Feminists have tried to ape men as a standard. This is unobtainable. In so doing, they have forsaken their own true feminism, which is a gift of God, and have gone after something which really does not exist and is totally unsatisfying. It is ruination for God's pattern of married life, and no marriage can succeed where such seeds are working in a woman's heart."

Fighting the wrong battles from wounded and crushed spirits and trying to become what we women are not leads to only one painful conclusion — further separation from one another. God never intended women to be like men or even for them to *try* to be like them. His creation of Eve out of relationship to Adam, and the giving back to Adam of Eve in relationship speak of a depth of outworking between two separate people, which it seems we have yet to see, in fullness, in relation to there being neither male nor female in the kingdom of God. In the meantime we are beginning to see the birth of established women's ministry.

General Eva Burrows does not regard herself as a feminist. She says, ''I feel that women have gifts from God, which they must use to His honour and glory. So I am not fighting for women to have a place, I just encourage women to use the gifts they have. I have grown up through the Salvation Army, where women are encouraged to have an identity of their own and feel that they have a valuable contribution to make. They do not need feminism. At both the ordained level and also at the local level we have women who are leading elders and women involved in decision-making. In our work in other countries too, such as Sri Lanka, many single women are recognised as officers and leaders, which is very unusual for Asian women.

''The feminist movements have sometimes gone wrong, putting men and women in competition with each other. But to be an equal does not mean you have to be the same. That famous quote from Matthew Henry sums it all up, when in essence he says that Eve was created from a bone in Adam, not from his head to be his boss nor from his foot to be his slave, but she was created from a bone in his side, to stand beside him, equal but different.

''It is interesting to note that Catherine Booth, our Army mother and wife of our founder, had seven children and was a great preacher. She challenged her own minister at the age of twenty-one, when he had implied that women were intellectually and morally inferior to men. Later she prepared a pamphlet called *Female Ministry*. At that point she was not a preacher, as she was rather a shy woman. She became aware, however, as God challenged her on her writing about women in ministry, when in fact she was not preaching herself. One day she interrupted her husband, saying, 'Can I have a word?' That was the beginning of her preaching ministry!

''She felt keenly on behalf of women at large, when many of the objections to the ministry of women, in her day, were based at best on nothing more substantial than convention and at worst on uninformed prejudice. This ignores the creative purpose of God, which was to make not two varieties of human beings but one. 'Male and female He created them, and He blessed them and named them man when they were created' (Genesis 5:2, RV). She also felt that Galatians 3:28 shows that there is to be no longer any distinction between Jew and Greek, slave and free, male and female.

''Catherine had a piercing intellect and was logically minded, being more intelligent than her husband, which he admitted. She also spoke of women having a redemptive role in life, and said that it was therefore important that, to fulfil her role, a woman must allow God to enrich and extend her capacities and powers.''

So it would seem that, without being a feminist, but rather being a woman who follows where God leads and picks up the challenges that He lays before us, a woman is enabled by the Holy Spirit to move into the ministry and works that God has foreordained for her.

Jill Dann, who has a wide-ranging ministry, shares that she once called herself a feminist, but the word has now been taken up, particularly by the media and various groups, and used in a different way, one with which she does not identify. She explains, ''I realise the worth of each individual in God's eyes and for me 'feminism' is simply the outworking of that fact for women. To that extent I am still a feminist! I took on the role that was expected of me. I knew it was what my husband Tony wanted me to do. He had made sure that I was free to do it, and in fact has pushed and encouraged me further. As a result, I have done much more than I would have done on my own.

''Also, at that stage in my life I cheerfully took verses out of context in Scripture, and accepted them. I questioned some of them a little, but not to the extent that it worried me, because I did not have time. I still have not completely resolved some of the Scriptures. There is always more to learn. I do not have a black and white position. I have always believed in equality of opportunity. We women have been made equal, but different. God gives us all different gifts and they need to be used. I have had security in my relationship with God, with my husband, and with the world outside, and I was quite sure what God wanted me to do.

"I do want to test everything by Scripture, but not out of context. Certain principles are timeless, but other Scriptures have a particular application to a particular situation; for example, a woman should be modest in her dress in church, but what constitutes modesty today? As far as Christians are concerned, I do not feel that feminism, as understood today, stands up to the Bible. In Ephesians 5, our attitude to other people and how we treat one another is to be one of mutual submission. This must be our hallmark."

Pat Cook also declares that she is not a feminist in today's meaning of the word. She also develops the idea of mutual submission as a key and continues, "But neither do I believe in mock humility or a 'lying down in the dust' mentality. Within the context of mutual submission, amongst men and women in the Church, we all need to be able to confront in a right way. Women are often cowed, and then become too strong, taking a mile instead of a yard. It is better to speak when you have something to say, win respect and find the balance, rather than speak out of insecurity."

That there is a difference between men and women is not in doubt. Feminists would have us believe that it is only biological. Yet if each of us is a unique human being, fearfully and wonderfully made, we are all different in every way, with multitudes of gifts. To bring us together so that we can maximise these for God requires a further key. How do we outwork God's answer to feminism, which is mutual submission?

Anita Traynar shares how she sees the way forward

towards an integrated Church. "Within the Church there are those women who are militant for women in leadership and ministry. I do not really know if they are doing our cause any good. I think that they are playing into the hands of the men who are expecting trouble with their women. My attitude has always been to encourage the women around me to have a servant heart. If we are seen to serve, then the men's attitude towards us is different, because they are not then really believing that we want to usurp them. We just want to work alongside them in our rightful place.

"The women who are more militant give you the feeling that it is almost a take-over bid. They feel they have to go that far to prove their power. This leaves me uncomfortable, even though I work with some of them, and they are my friends. A submissive heart will win the day more than getting on our high horse and fighting for the cause."

Here then is another key — to have a servant heart whereby people are blessed by an attitude of care as well as honesty. In serving others in whatever way God gives us, if we follow Jesus' example, people will inevitably be drawn to us. Trust is slowly established and responsibility given. We then move on to begin to think about leadership.

Pat Tomlinson believes that women, like men, have the ability to move into leadership. She explains, "In feminism, I am never quite sure what those women mean. Christian feminists can say one thing, with which I can agree. But I might work it out differently from the way they might work it out. Women are on a pilgrimage to re-educate men in a sense. That obviously has to start with their own husbands.

"I think that wives have to be quite careful, in the context of feminism, in becoming what they want to be in the Lord. It is such potential dynamite to a marriage, if it is not handled carefully and at a pace with which the husband can cope. It is much better for a man to learn gradually through the way a wife handles these things. Judging the pace, asking the questions and submitting can all help a man learn what things work well. I wish more wives would get it right, because it is so sad when you see marriages fall apart for this particular reason. Satan can get in when things happen frustratingly slowly.

"I would in fact far rather a man preach about woman's liberation than a woman. At this present time, that still holds more authority. Not all the members of our team hold the same view as Dave. He believes there is no reason why women should not be in the ultimate position of leadership as elders in a fellowship. He treads carefully here, and must do until there is some measure of agreement. But everyone in the team agrees that women should be ministering; it is just the degree or extent to which they can do it over which there is some disagreement."

Finally, **Sally McClung** says that she is not a feminist, but she believes in being feminine. She feels that feminists today have taken an extreme position with which she does not agree. She continues, "I think it is important that Christian women do not come under this spirit of the world. Rather, we must be careful to find God's place in our female roles, particularly in the area of leadership. We need to be careful not to go to extremes, but rather to find the 'radical middle'. We shouldn't be harsh, nor just quiet and unassuming. We should step out into what God has for us and in this we must find God's balance.

"We can be a hundred per cent feminine as we move out in obedience and in leadership. If God opens the door for us to be leaders, we do not need to lay down our femininity. For years I have worked as part of our leadership team here in Amsterdam, which includes both men and women. For a while I was the only woman — now we have other women on the team too. One of my roles was in bringing this female perspective. Often the men just did not see things from the same point of view. In making decisions to do with our ministry, it was important for me to speak up and feel free to share my point of view. They needed that in the discussion, in order to bring perspective and balance. If I put down that area, I was missing some of the things that I believe God wanted me to bring into that forum. God created male and female; one without the other means a lack of the whole picture."

So the conclusion on this issue is that the root attitude of militant, grasping feminism today is wrong. We have a different Spirit, our roots are in another kingdom, one where love defers to the other person. Another thread also comes through in our discussion. Within the Church, male domination can leave women frustrated in their ability to express and live out all that is in their hearts.

What, then, is the Bible's attitude to women's function in relation to men? Male and female, as mankind, were created in God's image to rule over creation together. The woman was made for Adam to have a companion. The word in Hebrew is *ezer*, often translated as 'helpmate'. It is a word often used to describe God Himself, who is our 'helper'. There was, therefore, no question of an inferior role for the woman to play. In Eden there was mutuality and partnership. The fall led to hierarchy, and patriarchy became the consequence.

As God said, the woman would so desire her husband that he would rule over her. This is the first indication of male dominance and female subjection. The other factor was to be pain and suffering in childbirth. The man, as a result of sin, was to work and toil for food.

These patterns and stereotypes began to develop through the Old Testament, with the occasional woman shining through in some kind of liberation. We have Deborah, the prophetess, leading Israel into victory. We have Queen Esther, who altered the course of Jewish history. We have the 'good wife' of Proverbs 31, who was certainly not locked inside her home. She made money, bought land, and ran a business. Her home was the springboard for her to move out from and touch the world. She was not a threat to her husband, for he praised her.

These women were all women in relationship with God. They had faith and as such were waiting for redemption in Christ. Mary the mother of Jesus is another example. She did not receive her call through Joseph or her rabbi. In fact Joseph clearly took second place at this time. When Jesus came, He broke the curse of sin. He related to women radically. He gave new meaning to them and their lives time and again. Women who were treated almost as slaves found themselves loved for their own sake.

He started teaching women alongside the male disciples. As a result, Jesus, who ministered to male disciples, found that women were responding to Him. The fact that women were the first to witness to the resurrection must have placed them in a position of some respect in the New Testament Church. Paul does not, however, use women in 1 Corinthians 15 as witnesses, because it would not be official, as a woman's evidence was of little value and lacked official status.

The explosion that Jesus' revolutionary attitude to women produced in the early Church was remarkable. The women lived lives to the full. The dignity Jesus gave women is reflected in how high a profile they had in the early Church. They were involved in early missionary activity, gathered with the apostles in the upper room to pray. Their homes were being used for meetings; some prophesied and as they matured, some taught the way of the Lord, as in Acts 18:26.

Paul was teaching that, just as there was neither slave nor free, so there was neither male nor female in the kingdom of God (Galatians 3:28). He also taught in 2 Corinthians 5:16-17 that we are no longer to consider one another after the flesh, which must include gender. He viewed all those in Christ as new creations. This proclamation of spiritual equality gave rise to such freedom that Paul also had to teach the women that they should not throw away their veils, because people would think they had become prostitutes! (1 Corinthians 11:13)

New Testament women were realising that they were coheirs with the men and with Jesus. They knew now that the Jesus seated at the right hand of the Father was not just male, but rather the embodiment of all humanity. They knew that in His eyes they were as precious to Him as the men, and that He had released them from the curse placed on women!

So finally, what conclusions can be drawn about this whole issue? Firstly, it almost seems as though men have allowed feminism to develop, because they have encouraged male dominance and not permitted or given value, credence and place to women in life. There has been such an over-emphasis on the masculine, to the rejection of the feminine, that the feminists are now desperately trying to imitate men, rather than bring their true feminine gifts into life. This has been true also in the Church. We have been part of the problem. We need to see the restoration of true femininity with place being given to gift and ability.

Secondly, men and women do not have the same psyches. Carl Jung has said that, in taking steps towards female social independence, many women have done themselves psychic injury by imitating men, instead of fulfilling their true feminine nature. Women have a different psyche to men, and a different bundle of gifts and abilities is found in each individual woman. To be locked into a 'feminist' identity can suppress true 'femininity', which is in need of restoration and healing in many women. God has given each of us the personality that we need, for the work He has called us to do.

Thirdly, today there is also a pressure within the Church to push it in an 'anti-feminist' direction. Christians often see 'women's libbers' as immoral, dominating, strident and seeking self-fulfilment while aiming to overcome male dominance; rather than simply seeing the enemy at work amongst women who are hurting.

We know that heart attitudes of rebellion and hatred will never bring in the kingdom of God. Women moving independently of men cannot bring to us the whole heart of God. Neither will a male-dominated Church reach out to the whole of mankind. God is in the business of bringing men and women together in the kingdom. Romans 12:2 says, "Do not be conformed any longer to the pattern of this world [which can be either male dominance or feminist reaction], but be transformed by the renewing of your mind."

So men are not the problem to be done away with! Aggression, pride and selfishness do not need to be forever fought, nor forever humoured. We are not called to 'lie down and die', nor to be in a power struggle. Insecure 'macho' men need release too, as much as domineering women. God wants to deal radically with the life of a man and woman together in its outworking. It is not that a man works and the woman stays at home and that the one is set against the other.

Ever since the beginning men and women have been

searching for peace together, but it will only be found in the building of relationships based on creative confrontation, which is without repression. I believe that God wants homes where both men and women are taking responsibility, and where the stereotypes are laid to rest. God wants men and women together secure enough in Him, both able to do whatever the Holy Spirit is asking them to do today, as well as in the long term. He wants homes where a husband is secure enough for his wife to have fulfilment outside, in both the Church and the world as well as in serving him, homes where a wife can feel free to ask her husband for committed help, not just in an emergency, as well as being willing to lay down her life for her family.

We are all new creations, created for good works. We are all ambassadors for Christ. I believe that God wants Christian businesses that take account of both male and female abilities and are not just following the usual stereotypes, where the man is chairman and the woman is secretary, for the sake of it. He wants businesses run on the balance of logic and intuition, where we can say that in decision-making, "Here we are, men, women and God together working it out," serving one another.

I believe God ultimately wants an alternative society, where men and women together, bearing the image of God, show forth redemption. Without women functioning, half of society is immobilised. This society will not be a male-dominant society, with structures inaccessible to women, nor a female reactionary society, where men are excluded; rather it will be a society where aggression and dominance are not hallmarks, but where a mutual submission and yielding to one another, in service of one another, are the norm, so that each person's gifts and abilities can flower and flourish — a society that brings us back to Eden, through redemption, and where we can give something beautiful back to God.

Three

Submission

The word 'submission' means to yield and come under a certain control, or become subordinate to another. In the Garden of Eden, God intended the joint rule of creation by Adam and Eve. Sin entered in. One result was God's word that man would rule over woman, because her desire would be for her husband (Genesis 3:16). As a result the general expectation has been that women should submit to men. However, this was not what God originally intended; it was simply the result of sin.

In many cultures the place of women is inferior to men. This works through custom, tradition, and often law. Man was created before woman, therefore women, who have been thought of as secondary, are expected to submit to men. One has to ask the question that if the order of creation is so crucial, is man secondary to the animals, who were created before him?

The answer is obvious, yet the stereotypes persist. As God said that the consequence of sin would turn 'joint rule' into the woman being 'ruled over' by the man, this has worked out as the woman continually turning towards her husband, as she turns away from God. So we have seen women consistently submitting, often to the point of wrongly laying down their very selves over issues, until we have things like the battered wife syndrome, where a woman is conditioned to do nothing except fearfully accept continual physical abuse. Dying to self does not mean dying to our being and doing.

This is not godly submission. Eve was given as a helper to Adam who, when he was alone, was incomplete. The word 'helpmate' means 'a companion in the same work'. She was meant to complement him, and he her. If we consistently talk about submission as the woman's subordinate role, we will end up with women submerged completely, if they do not rebel. Their lives will be lived through the lives of their men and, without a positive contribution of their own, women in the Church become passive and just somebody else's wife, or they rage at the frustrations and injustices of a lack of clear feminine identity and function.

In the Church this has been a contentious issue now for some time. Some women can spend years getting themselves to be what they think it is to be submissive. Many become passive and dull doormats in the effort, and wrongly depend on their husbands to make every decision for them. Others find themselves called rebellious because they still know that they have a valid opinion, and will not silently suppress it, expecting their husbands to take account of it in joint decision-making. The whole issue seems to be a catch-22 situation. If you submit, you become submerged and lose some of the colour of your personality. If you do not submit, you are considered a rebellious woman who is strong and opinionated.

In some groups within the Church head covering is a major issue. Women must be responsible to men: to their husbands if married and to a male leader or married couple if single. The outward sign of this is the wearing of a hat or headscarf in the public meeting. To outsiders that is strange, especially within our culture. In 1 Peter 3:6, Peter shows how Sarah, within her culture, showed her submission to Abraham by calling him her master. Today in our culture, if women start speaking in this way, will it be what God intended for us? Has the Holy Spirit more to say to us today on the issue of submission? What does the word submission really mean in its outworking and is there any significance today concerning head covering?

Sylvia Mary Alison's history in regard to this issue is interesting. She explains, ''My husband was brought up in a strictly evangelical tradition, which was very male-oriented. He was converted through John Stott and was a counsellor at All Souls for many years. For him it was all very rational. I am not a rational sort of person, rather an intuitive one. So when we heard about the gifts of the Holy Spirit in the sixties, I was filled with the Spirit and speaking in tongues, and getting words from the Lord about things which my husband could not accept were God's ideas.

"Sometimes I had an impression of something I thought the Lord wanted me to do, but my husband would say 'no', because it did not make sense to him, as it was not easily verifiable. I would then cry out to the Lord, 'What am I to do? It seems You are telling me to do this, but my husband says 'no'.' Yet the whole of the time it was as if the Lord was saying, 'Obey your husband, don't do anything without his consent, and then, when he consents, it is a seal to it, because I have put him in authority over you.' And so my intuitive gifts were not just irrational outbursts, but were submitted to my husband's mind.

"For several years I did this very painfully, often feeling I did not do things God wanted me to do. I told the Lord that if He wanted me to obey my husband, He must change his mind! This came into focus when we started Prison Fellowship. At that moment, my husband saw what I was doing, he gave his consent and was my covering in it. So in 1978 I became Chairman and leader of Prison Fellowship. Now today it is different, in that my husband is more able to accept things, because he gets words too! We move forward together, much more strongly than if I had gone off on my own saying, 'Well I'm going to do my own thing anyway.'

"At the same time, the Lord taught me further when I was invited on to the Nationwide Initiative on Evangelism committee. I do not find committees easy, but the Lord said to me that in the Body of Christ, the women are the heart and the men are the head. The heart pumps blood around the body and ventilates the body, but the head sends the signals to the body as to what to do. The heart gives the energy to the body to do those things. So we have different functions, equally valuable. A committee with all men is very cerebral, they come up with bright ideas and administrative thoughts, but they do not come up with the way something feels, for example with God's grief about something, with which I am more in tune.

"On the committee for the Nationwide Initiative on Evangelism, I was one of two women amongst many men. I needed to bring and submit my insights and feelings which needed thought, before deciding what to do concerning them. I was under the decision-making of the committee. Some of the men were not used to a woman with such insights — the sort of women who sat on committees with them were women who thought like men and behaved in an administrative manner.

"I coped with some of the non-acceptance similarly to when I was on the board of Spree '73, when I was also just one of two women amongst many men. I was terrified and really frightened even of speaking, so much so that I really got into an enormous knot. At one board meeting I burst into tears, because I was so tongue-tied. I was expected to say something and I felt a failure. It seemed that no one really understood what I was doing, and in fact I had failed to explain it.

"I talked to Jean Darnall, who was involved with a prayer group that I belonged to. She ministered to me, and set me free from a root of fear of men. This was rooted in my need to please my father, when I was at school. He was always saying, 'Well, next term you will do better,' but I never did. I was afraid I would not come up to expectations, became tongue-tied and it came to a crunch at this board meeting. Things then changed for me; for example I was no longer tense before a board meeting.

"So, on the committee for the Nationwide Initiative on Evangelism, five years later, I wondered if it would all be the same again, but I found I was not frightened. It was through their courtesy towards me that this time I was more courageous, able to say things and able to confess in one of our devotions that I had always been frightened of men, but I had now found I was not any more, through my healing. We were together for one day a month for three years. They made me leader of the devotions, the prayer bit, and I had to appoint one of them each time to lead according to their churchmanship.

"I am not afraid of submitting to men because I feel free.

The Bible asks us to submit to one another, whether man or woman, but especially I expect them if necessary to submit to me. For instance, in Prison Fellowship, I am the Chairman. There are no other women on the board. My executive director is a man. I do not believe in being authoritarian; I like to discuss the issues and hear from the members of the board the good ideas that we can take up. I never wanted to be in this position and it took me a long time to be happy in the role. I was very surprised to be made Chairman and would be very happy for someone else to take it on, but I do believe God has put me there to do a job.''

Eileen Vincent does not believe Scripture means that all women submit to all men. She comments, ''In the Church, all people submit to all people. We are a submitted company. Also, wives are called to submit to their husbands. That does not mean wives obey. The Scripture says children and slaves obey, but wives should submit. The old-fashioned Anglican service has caused a discredit there, because submission is different from obedience, and we need to take note of that, although they are closely linked.

''Those who know me tell me that I'm a very strong character. In most people's thinking, a strong character was synonymous with lack of submission. This used to scare me to death as a Christian woman. I would be frightened of myself and say to God that I was not what I felt I ought to be. I really had a hate campaign against myself. Then the Lord did a most incredible thing for me. I was at a leaders' and wives' meeting and they announced the subject — 'Submission'! I couldn't bear the thought, and then the opening words of Arthur Wallis, who was speaking, were, 'The foundation for submission is the acceptance of yourself, and if you do not accept yourself you are fighting against the creation of God. God created you and then He said that He is pleased with you!'

''This came to me like a shot from heaven and was the truth that set me free. From that day on I went to work on really coming to terms with myself, never wishing I was somebody else again. I began to thank the Lord that He had made me, me. He had not made a mistake by giving me a strong character and my kind of gifts. I put all those wrong thoughts to death and would no longer sin with wrong attitudes. From then on I just knew a total peace inside. Failure to accept myself and the kind of person I was had deep roots in me. These problems had only happened since I had become a Christian. It was the guilt or condemnation that comes upon many women, which is frankly a religious thing. I had never understood what was wrong.

"I am married to a leader who is submitted to other leaders. We have not allowed my husband's relationships to muddle our relationship. I am submitted to those over me in the Church, and to my husband. The Scripture says 'Submit to those over you in the Lord,' and I do that from the bottom of my heart. I do it also where the person over me is a young man whom I've nurtured in the Lord and who has grown up with the anointing of God coming upon him. I then happily submit to him."

In Philippians 2:6-8, we see Jesus submitting to become like us. He did not grasp at equality with God. Jesus was strongly submissive. It is not a weak verb. But it also stems back to a relationship with God. If we are, like Him, secure and fulfilled in our relationship with the Father, we do not have a major problem in this area, nor in working out this principle in our various relationships.

Valerie Griffiths shares from Scripture: "Several words are used to describe the relationship between believers. In Ephesians 5:21, all are to be subject to one another, including wives to their husbands. Gilbert Bilezikian, in *Beyond Sex Roles*, points out that only equals can be subject to each other. No officer can subject himself to his men. This mutual submission pattern is extended to wives and husbands in marriage and is the submission of servanthood.

"The Greek word for 'submit' is *hupotasso*. It is a military word meaning 'to rank under'. In battle the infantry interlocked their shields against the enemy, and they stood together in order. All Christians, including wives, are to work together in this way. There is no place for individuals to demand their own rights and whims. The individuals subject themselves to others.

"Arndt and Gingrich in their Greek lexicon describe submission as 'voluntary yielding in love'. It is a gift a wife offers her husband, not a right the husband can ever demand of his wife. It is offered to persons worthy of respect. Gretchen Gaebelein Hull, in *Equal to Serve*, points out that *hupertasso* is also used for attaching documents to each other. As a husband is told to leave his parents and cleave to his wife, so she is told to attach herself to him. Again there is mutuality.

"Women are commanded to respect their husbands, (Ephesians 5:33), men are commanded to love their wives, (Ephesians 5:25), and to honour them (1 Peter 3:7). Each is to give themselves in servanthood to the other. When Paul talks of a husband as 'head' of the wife, he goes on to describe Christ as the 'head' of the Church, her Saviour. If head had meant authority and rule, Christ would have been described as Lord.

"As Paul expressed it the pattern for a husband's love is the total self-denying, self-giving love of Christ, the saviour and servant, laying down His life for the Church. Here, hierarchy, rule and authority (the last never mentioned of marriage except in 1 Corinthians 7:4, where husband and wife each have authority over the other) have no place. Elaine Storkey, in *What's Right with Feminism*, has said, 'The way others will know we are Christ's disciples is in the way we love one another, and not in the way we exercise authority over one another.'

"As far as head covering is concerned, it is not an issue for me. When you look at the Greek text, it is so obscure, it says nothing about hats, nor even about veils, but rather something hanging down, and then refers to long hair as a covering, in 1 Corinthians 11:15. Dr W.J. Martin suggests it was the shaved heads of the converted prostitutes which were offensive.

"Living in Japan, we found it was inappropriate to ask the women to wear hats. You cannot wear a hat or any other head covering with a kimono. If they cover their heads with a scarf while dusting, they remove it out of respect and politeness if a visitor comes to the door. If it was a sign in Corinth of being under authority, it does not have that significance today. When I covered my head in Singapore, I did it in submission to the elders, because they were the church leaders and I did not feel it was my place as an overseas guest to be different.''

Grace Barnes feels clearly too that the Scripture says that we should submit to one another, both men and women. She explains further meaning to the Greek word *hupotasso*. *Hupo* means 'under', and *tasso* means 'to arrange'. The context in Ephesians 5 is marriage and a woman is not to assert her rights, but rather yield to her husband.

''Let's consider Adam and Eve in Genesis 1:26-27. They were put in the garden as equals. But God only told Adam about the tree of good and evil. He did not tell Eve. In this I see that what God wanted was not for Adam to lord it over Eve, but rather it was as though God was saying to Adam, 'Look after Eve and care for her, making sure that she does not eat of that tree, because it will not do her good.' As I see it, Adam could not have been around when Satan came to Eve; they were both enjoying doing what they each enjoyed doing, and were not necessarily together all the time.

''To me submission is all about my husband caring for me and loving me so much that he does not want any harm to come to me. I can submit to that. Personally, when my husband Norman is travelling, I choose to submit to other people, because I want to be cared for while he is away, by men or women, according to the situation at the time.

''Headcovering for me is my husband, who cares for me, or anyone around at the time that I submit to in given situations. As far as the Scriptures are concerned, we need to look at the situation, culture and time. How they behaved wrongly in this area at that time would for us today be the equivalent of a woman showing her underwear or breasts.''

The issue of headcovering in the Church today is a diverse one. In many churches it is part of the expected normal female dress, whether hat or headscarf. To some groups it is the sign of the submission of women. In some meetings, where the church streams are mixed, you see some women, when they want to pray or prophesy, getting out a three-cornered scarf and putting it on their heads. To others it seems completely incongruous and can become one of those side-issues which could divide us.

Some ladies have humorous stories to relate in relation to headcovering, for example being the only woman present in a meeting without one and the issue being preached at her from the pulpit; in another instance, deciding to remove an uncomfortable hat only to find that another lady in the same meeting decided to do the same thing, at the same time! Wondering if they were rebellious, both ladies found freedom.

In the Salvation Army it is part of their uniform, which is not complete without a head-piece. However, in some parts of the world they wear a hat, but in other parts they wear nothing on their heads, as in India, Indonesia and the Philippines, where culturally hats are not worn.

A headcovering is a thing that some have never felt comfortable wearing, but did so because it was expected. It is one of those things you can do and yet your heart may be a million miles away from the right attitude, far from submissive. It is also one of those things where, if there really is spiritual significance, God will surely restore it to the whole Church in a real and living way, as we walk with Him.

Pat Cook, who is a single woman in ministry, feels that a submissive heart is very important. ''I am not married, but am covered by a leadership team of men and women, and I would submit to them and their decisions even if I did not necessarily agree with them. For example, I will say strongly if I feel and think they are wrong. However, the end result is that they see I will submit to them, in what they ultimately decide.

''When I am asked to speak, I speak forthrightly, to men and women, from where I am at. Submission does not mean that you cannot say things, cannot argue, and cannot move out. I say this carefully; often a woman is not given the platform, because she has got something to say which challenges the men, and the men are threatened, not knowing how to handle it.

"I remember one committee I sat on where, when the coffee came in, the men all looked at me, the only woman, to pour out the coffee, because I was a woman. I made the decision not to pour. But God spoke to me about my attitude. Now I pour out the coffee, not out of submission to them, but in order to serve. In fact, there is a race to the trolley in order to do that!

"I am now much more confident, in my own position of leadership, to correct if I feel someone is saying something wrong. I am often asked, 'Pat, what do you think about this?' and I can say what I feel. When I first came into leadership, I found it very hard. I felt second-class, but as I learned to be submissive, this attitude has been the key to my development. When people find you are not a bossy woman, they ask you back again. And I will go back to encourage the women out into what God has for them, and to challenge people on world mission. Submission is not for women only in the Church — we all need this attitude towards one another!"

Patricia Higton has come to see that it is important in God's kingdom that there is a certain order. She explains, "I'm not sure that we understand fully all the reasons for submission. I have come to realise lately that it has something to do with the next life as well as this life. It also has something to do with being under authority, and following through by exercising authority oneself. God is training us to reign with Him in the next life. There will be positions of authority and we are being trained here, in a certain order, learning about His Lordship, about submitting to rulers in the secular realm, and about Church order. The relevant Scriptures here would be Hebrews 13:17 and Romans 13:1.

"These things do not come easily, particularly to someone with leadership gifts. I know that the more free I become, and the more I exercise leadership myself, the more I feel the need for protection in my own leadership. I receive this from the two men who are elders in my Church, one of whom is my husband. I also know that within that there is all the freedom that I could ever wish for, to serve God.

"At home, Tony and I just basically function as equals. We

also have our different spheres of leadership, with different gifts and ministries, yet I do sense a need for protection, the more I go out on a limb. I have never found the matter of submission an easy one, and I cannot bear any concept of women being treated as inferior or as doormats, and not being set free to exercise their gifts and ministries.

"A lot of men who get it wrong in the Church also get it wrong at home, and their wives can be treated almost like slaves, which was never meant to be. Where men have to keep talking about their authority and their wives' submission, there is something wrong somewhere."

The issue of slavery is in fact worthy of note. Wilberforce, who fought so hard to break down slavery, is admired. Today there is a need for women to be free to move into what God intends for them. Paul tells slaves to submit to masters; he did not say that they should break away and get free. The issues are comparable. Do we, therefore, believe that we should still have slaves today? Because we question the cultural situation regarding women's place, this in no way means we are questioning the heart of the gospel. We need to remember that the Holy Spirit is still revealing things to us today. Paul never said the final word on everything.

Myra Blyth things that submission of women to men in general does not stand up to scrutiny. She says, "If you look at Paul's quote on wives submitting to husbands in context, he is talking about the mutual submission of men to women and women to men. It is a unique partnership, which I believe is what Paul is aiming at. Paul talks about the role of women in the Church in different contexts and different ways. He did not say to women, 'Don't speak in church'; he said, 'Cover your heads.' When he said, 'Ask your husband at home,' it was because of the chaos going on in the service itself. There has to be an integrity about the Bible tradition and enough has been said to show that women should not be silent, 'submissive' and invisible!

"Emotionally I feel that to say that women should submit to men is a subversive ploy on the part of men who want to maintain the status quo, and use the Bible to help them do so, saying that women should be in submission to men. It is part of a whole superstructure within some elements of the Church, which has been set up to promote a certain ideology on the place of the family, of women and right morals, an ideology which is there to suit the convenience of those who constructed it.

"Finally I feel that to say that women should be in submission to men does not stand up in terms of real relationships. I had a friend who was a house-group leader. She felt guilty that it was not her husband who was leading it. She tried so hard to hand it over to her husband and to say nothing more. My heart bled for her.

"I do not understand why we are diminishing the very gifts and skills and vocation of an individual, because somebody somewhere has decided Paul's teaching on women being silent should be observed! The inconsistencies are phenomenal. The idea that women can teach children, who are open and vulnerable to the truth, but cannot teach those who are supposedly mature and wise, is a total inconsistency. The idea that women can teach on the mission field because there are no men, but not in England, is hypocrisy.

"When Robert and I are looking at an issue, we mutually respect each other's gifts and skills and insights. He is very good in the area of administration and finances, but he would not then go off and make the financial decisions alone — we work the budget together. We argue the detail; because there is a morality, a life style and a faith behind every decision, and we would want to come to a common decision.

"I believe it is possible to have a mutual agreement. You can end up saying that you have some reservations, but in the light of what is said, and because of the reasons given, you will go along this path. I cannot imagine that God intends that at the end of a very long debate my husband should say, 'Well I think that you've got some very sound arguments there, but I am the man and my arguments win!' The issue for me is not *who* makes the decision, it is rather *how* we make the *right* decision, in the best of what we know, and by the grace of God, He will go with us in the decision we have made."

Marriage can be said to be like a journey on a motorway together. The husband might be driving making the decisions to turn the wheel, but both are constantly feeding each other information about the journey and the right turnings. Eventually, yes, he makes the turn, but it's all by mutual discussion, with joint decision-making and not just the wife feeding the husband information for him to make every decision. Life is like this too, and in that context, it should be a rare thing to say, 'Right, this is what I am going to make us do!'

Ruth Calver says she finds it hard to submit to men who are not being men. She continues, ''I can happily submit to anyone in the area of gifting, whether it is male or female, or people who are working in an area in which I have no experience or ability, expecially when I see what the Lord has done in them and how He is using them. In my marriage, which is a partnership, when we have prayed and talked about something and not come to an agreement, I will submit to my husband, as the Scripture asks me to. This is not just for the sake of it, because 'the man's the man and we women must submit', which does not seem credible to me. Headcovering was to a large extent a cultural outward expression of submission. A similar token for us today would be our wedding ring. Personally, I don't refuse to wear a headcovering in rebellion, I just do not feel it is an issue.''

From her experience as a doctor, **Anne Townsend** feels that submission means that the person who is best trained tells the other what to do, regardless of their sex. She comments, ''In the context of the Church, I am helped by concepts of mutual submission, man to woman and woman to man. Given the right kind of leadership from a woman, I am very happy with it.

''Sometimes women opt out of the responsibility over something that God has given them to do, saying, 'I won't do such and such, because I am submitting to the man who is covering me.' Some of us are going to be answerable for our actions, because we were given responsibility and we abdicated from it. We need to watch that we don't fall into that trap. It makes life so easy to put our brains away in a little box and say to God, 'OK, I won't do any thinking or agonising or praying about this thing, I'll submit it to a man and do what he tells me to do.'

"If I disagree with a man whom I am working with over an important matter, then I want to share and explain my feelings and ask him to tell me how he came to his conclusions. When necessary I would want to confront him, as I would similarly want to do with a woman! In the past I have been more fearful of a man's power than I need have been, and I have excused myself with Bible texts out of context. A man cannot be presumed to be right simply because he is genetically male! I am not wrong automatically, just because I have a female body, and female hormones!

"It is important in relating, especially when disagreeing, that a man and a woman understand one another. If, having each seen the other's point of view, we still disagree, I would very much want to have the grace to be able to say that I still cannot agree, but will be in there behind him and trust that God will bless and work through it. I would want to pray for the person throughout, and would promise not to gossip, considering the matter closed.

"Once a male colleague and I disagreed. We talked and struggled to understand each other. The outcome was that we are now able to work very closely together. God took that disagreement to make a relationship between us that can stand a lot of strain. From my perspective we spent a weekend wasting our time, talking and sharing. Now, however, he knows where I am coming from. He operates on an intellectual thinking level and understands that I operate at a feeling level, which he doesn't write off, as he used to. So we respect one another's differences and can complement one another."

When we place value on one another, submission becomes easier. If we lack those values, abuse takes place. Some women find themselves in very difficult positions today with unhappy marriages, where the husband beats them and they have to submit to his beatings. Without advocating divorce, we should not expect women to suffer and be abused until they are crushed. What sort of God are we portraying in this, or is our idea of Him one of hardness and punishment? It takes faith and love to make a relationship work and individual counselling is needed to help hear what the Holy Spirit is saying in a given situation.

So often guilt is heaped onto the situation. If a marriage is not working and if we have in our thinking a strong headship (dominance) and submissive (subservience) theology, then we always fall short of the mark. This causes feelings of loneliness, anger and guilt which are often suppressed instead of expressed, leading to more guilt. We must not idolise maleness and undermine femaleness.

Marion White shares from her experience, when Rob and she were in 'Open House'. ''We often took in young men who had been brought up in children's homes. They would often have an in-built hatred of women. They had matronly women in the homes and had often been abused by women. One in particular would hardly recognise a woman. His sole target in our house was me, because he saw that I too was quite a strong character, not meek and mild and quiet. I was a real threat to him. He was a Christian, and his belief was that all women submitted to all men. So we had big clashes!

''I always used to point this chap back to the verse in Ephesians that talks about us submitting to one another in the Lord. I feel that unless you are married, you submit to each other, as men and women together out of respect. A woman does not have to submit automatically to every man going, without having that same response from them!

''Eventually I got through to him, but what was exciting was that in the end, when we were leaving Crawley, we had a meeting to say goodbye. People were praying with us and this chap actually stood up and read a Psalm for me. It was really moving as it was at that point that I realised that we had actually made it, and now had a good relationship. But it had taken a long time for his prejudices to go because he had been very hurt. He has since married, which is indicative of the fact that he has come through his problem in relating to women.

''Obviously, in the Church context, we are meant to submit

to those in authority over us, both men and women. We need to be led by those divinely appointed to be our leaders. But I suppose one of the things that has happened to us over the last few years is that we have become like sheep, perhaps because of a heavy authority or shepherding principle that has been taught. In some quarters it has almost got to the point where you miss out God and just go to your leader and he will tell you what to do. Women particularly have taken that almost as an easy way out, without having to develop their own relationship with God. I am very happy to submit to a man who I know is really wanting the best for me, and is guiding and advising me. There is a happy submission, and I'm sure it is meant to be a two-way thing.''

Jean Darnall feels a woman inherently has an attitude of needing a man's authority around her. She continues, ''Usually a daughter and her father are closer than a daughter and a mother. It is just something in our nature. We want a man who knows what he is doing, has authority, is protective, and will provide for us. It is all in our need as women.

''In working for the Lord, I have been in such situations as when, for instance, for about six years my husband was teaching in college in a whole different arena to me. I was on the pastoral staff of Angelus Temple in the U.S., the only woman on the ministerial staff where there were five leading pastors. I wanted the head pastor to be the head and I did not want the responsibility. But on the other hand, in my own area of services and duties I wanted to lead.

''This worked through mutual submission. I submitted to the head pastor and the other pastors in the overall planning, policy and decision-making, but in the area of my responsibility, they submitted to me. It was not a competitive thing, but very cooperative. I submitted also to my husband, who was overall head of that staff. If he told me, 'No, I don't want you to do that,' then I would take that to my head pastor and tell him that Elmer did not want me to do that, for whatever reason. He might have felt it was not within my energy or my calling. It would have been accepted as pretty final.

''Before Elmer and I married, we discussed our ministries and our callings. Elmer, at one time after our son was born, when I became quite ill with low thyroid deficiency, saw me losing inspiration and becoming depressed. I wanted to quit, and told him, 'You go ahead and be the pastor and I will just be the pastor's wife.' I remember that for a couple of days he worked at it, but was really troubled. Finally, he said that before he married me, he covenanted with the Lord that he would never do anything to interfere with God's calling in my life. As my husband he did not want to be guilty of interfering with my ministry. When you have that kind of understanding, it takes care of the problem.

''In Paul's time, in the New Testament, a woman that would not submit to her husband was up for divorce. I think that Paul was addressing more the problem of divorce of the marriage, than a ministry problem. When Elmer and I have had disagreements on guidance from the Lord, or on where to go or minister, it has developed for us that I would do what Elmer said. The ideal is where we agree, but the few times when this has occurred and I submitted, invariably it was right, and God honoured that and worked it out to His glory.''

Submission, therefore, comes out of friendship and respect. Wives actually do have an opinion for husbands to listen to. Provided that her husband has heard her viewpoint, and really heard it and not just fobbed her off, most ladies are happy for husbands to make a final decision. Submission also starts with relationship rather than roles, although there is a place for roles in marriage relationships, to maintain order and avoid confusion. The more maturity there is in the relationship between the husband and wife, or co-workers, the less need there is for roles and the more each will depend on working in partnership. Each partnership varies and through the years communication is developed as best suits each, with husbands making some decisions, while in other areas of life it is the wife who makes decisions.

Christine Noble concludes by pointing out that nowhere in the Bible do we see the principle that all women should submit to all men. ''These words refer to wives submitting to their husbands. This is to do with the social order, rather than the Church order. If my social order is sorted out and my walk with my husband is good, then when I come into the Church, if I hold office and he does not, he can submit to me.

''The mistake we have made in the past is to bring this aspect of social order into the Church, and it is the only bit we try to bring in. We do not for example try to bring in employer and employee submission, when they come into the Church. The office manager does not automatically have authority over the filing clerk. I believe that it should be the same for husbands and wives as well. Social status should not automatically be a part of Church order.

''A wife must be submissive in the social order to her husband, but in the Church she must be submissive to the order of the Church and ideally there should be no conflict. This has often become cloudy, because sometimes the husband is also an elder or leader and the wife is seen submitting there, but I believe we will increasingly see the reverse in the Church, where the wife is seen as a leader and the husband is seen to be submitting to that, within the Church order.

''I believe everyone should have a heart of submission to one another and to one another's gifts and that has nothing to do with sex. It is the way that God wants us to live our lives out in the Church. So, when people in the world look at us, they see peace and calm at the heart of our Church order, and there is calm and security in our social order too.''

It is not unknown now to find within some House Churches a wife who is on the local leadership team, whose husband is not a leader. Submission can work happily, even in what might be a difficult area. The wife can lead in every area, except her marriage, with her husband quite happy to follow her lead in terms of church meetings and church life. But in terms of their marriage, he leads. The leadership needs first to ask him if he is happy that some of her time be given to lead the church, because it will take time from the marriage. Having agreed to this, he too can now recognise the call to leadership upon his wife's life. We all need to be able to follow and be able to submit, especially if we aspire to leadership, for it is in submitting that we are given authority.

In learning the principle mistakes are often made. A baby learns to walk by falling over. When God was restoring this principle of submission many women submitted to any man. It did not seem to matter whether you had a relationship with that man or not, whether marriage or friendship. It was not something openly taught, but rather something that happened. Today, in many fellowships, a more balanced approach is to be found and single women with a heart attitude of submission find they do not have to submit to every man who comes across their path.

In conclusion then, we can say that Christians first need to look to Jesus to see what true submission really is. Jesus knew who He was: the Son of God from heaven. He knew why He was born into this world: in order to be its Saviour. He then willingly laid down His life. In a clear choice, He submitted Himself to His Father's will. This absolute submission belongs only to God. Jesus is our pattern. He submitted Himself out of a right fear of God.

The Scriptures also talk about many other kinds of submission: to one another, to authority, the younger to the elder, yet we have, in this generation in the Church, overly stressed just one submission, that of wives to husbands. This has produced a mindset whereby, if a man is always to be over a woman, whenever he serves her, he will do it as a favour. Similarly, if a woman is always under a man's authority, she will always serve him feeling there is no choice. What God requires of us all is a submissive heart.

Many women today have so very little to lay down. They don't know who they are. They don't know what they are here for. If all you have is negative feelings about yourself, there is very little positive that you can lay down. So the primary issue in submission must be that you have something positive to submit! Many women need personal healing in this whole area of feminine identity in order to become maturely able to submit at all.

Then we need to have something or someone to submit to. If we look at the women in Scripture who related to Jesus, we can see that His revolutionary attitude towards them allayed all their fears. His attitude first of all was to lift women to the status of people in their own right, after centuries of slave-like living. This so set women free to be who God intended them to be, that their response out of such heartfelt gratitude and love could only be to lay down their very lives for this man. This was their inner response of love and held no fear whatsoever. This was true submission.

The Scripture asks wives to submit to their husbands in this way, "as unto the Lord". We, therefore, also need to consider whom we are to submit to, as wives. A wife in the Church is to submit to a husband, who "loves her and gives himself up for her, just as Christ loved the Church". Being vulnerable and open and allowing others to be part of our life gives protection.

The issue of headship is beautifully dealt with in 1 Corinthians 11, yet some misunderstandings as to what is meant by 'headship' occur because of the way the Greek word *kephale* is translated. It means the head or cornerstone, but also the source, origin or beginning. So we can get different opinions on headship. In English the word 'head' has the connotation of authority such as ruler, boss or chief. However, in ancient times, the heart was considered to be the source of thought and emotions; but 'head' was 'the source of life'. As a result, many Greek scholars have not found the meaning of *kephale* or 'headship' to be 'having authority' or 'controlling'. Rather they have found it to mean 'source of life'.

Men are to love their wives, as Christ loved the Church, which is a terrific thing to ask of them. The man's relationship to his wife is therefore that of a servant. This is a husband's true submission. Greek men had not been used to loving their wives. They were no longer to treat their wives as chattels. Paul also told people who owned slaves that they must be patient and just. Wives had to be respectful, not aggressive, and slaves had to be obedient. We do not find this passage saying that women should just obey men and not take initiative.

In Ephesians 5:23, there is something of the attitude that the husband 'saves' his wife. This headship is one of real care rather than control. God looks to the husband to be responsible rather than having totalitarian authority. He needs to liberate his wife and bring her into freedom. Heavy authority can very often mean insecurity.

In Colossians 3:19, Paul does not allow harsh treatment of wives by husbands. Rather he wants women to discover their true identity and vocation, as men have done. This however is not to be done in isolation. Eve needed Adam as much as Adam needed Eve! A mutual submission is to be outworked.

So, we find Paul writing to people in Greek culture, where Greek women were almost never allowed out and certainly not to speak in public. A wife was somebody special and kept separate. The possibility of a wife speaking in public was unthinkable. Yet in 1 Corinthians 11:10, the woman is to have a sign of authority on her head. This must mean what it says. She must now have authority, to move up alongside the men to pray and prophesy within the submitted company, and to function as a full member of the body of Christ, rather than to be up in the gallery chattering, as the Jewish women would have been in the synagogue.

Bilezikian in *Beyond Sex Roles* says that he feels that this command was written to oppose the misinformed zeal of Judaic misogynists (women-haters), who were trying to impose repressive rules, designed to restrict female participation in the life of the Church. Submission per se is not to be used as an excuse to restrict women. If women are not to exercise authority, as Paul says in 1 Timothy 2:12, it means the kind of authority that is domineering and usurping — *authentes*. This behaviour is always wrong, not just in marriage.

Bilezikian also moves away from the hierarchical view of the text, to the more natural chronological view.

"In verse 3, Paul begins with Christ/man (creation of man), which in a hierarchical structure should be second. He goes on with man/woman (formation of woman), which in a hierarchical structure should be third. Then he ends up with God/Christ (birth of Christ), which in a hierarchical structure should be first. It is inconceivable that Paul would have so grievously jumbled up the sequence in a matter involving God, Christ and humans, when he kept his hierarchy straight as he dealt with the lesser subject of spiritual gifts in 1 Corinthians 12:28!''

Finally, the whole issue of submission must be summed up in Ephesians 5:21: ''Submit to one another out of reverence for Christ.'' We are all to submit to one another's gift. But how does a husband submit to his wife? By loving her as Christ loved the Church and laying his life down for her! And how does a wife submit to her husband? By responding and loving him in the way that she respects and loves Jesus. Just as Jesus came to serve rather than to be served and to lay His life down, so everyone who has this attitude of submission — husbands and wives, ministers and congregations, will in the end not lose their life, but rather find it.

Mutual submission is one of the paradoxes of the kingdom of God and takes us back to the Garden of Eden, showing us what God really intended in the relationship between Adam and Eve. God has taken the wrong submission of women to men, which is the result of the fall, and within the Body of Christ has released women along with men to have heart attitudes of true submission. We must, therefore, begin to take this ground back, starting where God calls us, in our homes first and then in the Church, in order that the Holy Spirit can show the world what God really intended. Truly biblical submission has far-reaching implications.

SECTION 2

OLD CHESTNUTS

Four

Deception

Deception implies trickery. Often, people who move into spiritual deception do so gently and quietly, but the result is often that another 'split' takes place in God's Church. Satan does not deceive us with a great show of noise. Eve was tricked by a subtle snake, whispering in her ear. It is interesting that she was not surprised that the serpent spoke!

Deception means ultimately to disobey God, and failure to seek the Lord concerning the consequences. Eve knew she had been deceived — she admitted it. Adam angrily blamed Eve for his sin, and God for giving him this woman who had caused his sin! Traditionally, Eve had been held responsible for bringing sin into the world. Her deception has implied moral, intellectual and emotional weakness and women have been equated with temptation, deception and manipulation through the ages. We have already seen some quotations from the early Church fathers, who seemed to hate women as much as some of the Jews had done in history.

The well-known Scripture in 1 Timothy 2:14 is the only one in the New Testament that is directed towards women, but there are many Scriptural warnings given by Jesus and Paul, about taking heed that no man deceive us! Yet so often we hear that women are the more easily deceived. So what is the Holy Spirit saying to us today? What do leading Christian women in our generation feel about this issue, in the light of the fact that most of the large sects and world religions have been started by men?

Pat Tomlinson remembers hearing, in the past, statements about 'deception' being a woman's weakness. She shares what she now thinks. "I feel it is absolute rubbish to say that women are more open to deception than men. Dave has just written a paper on the whole subject of women and has read many books on this. His background means that although he feels instinctively that something is wrong in this concept, just by the general feel of Scripture, he has to actually sift through the Scriptures to be able to convince himself and our team what the truth is. So he has gone into this in a big way, and finds no grounds for this statement at all." (See Conclusion.)

Rosemary Andrews shares how it always baffles her as to why some people are so easily led astray. She continues, "There seems to be so little discernment around in the Church. Pride, rejection and control are often at the root of a person entering deception. Someone once said to me, 'When your piece of truth becomes "the truth, the whole truth, and nothing but the truth", you are on the road to deception!' Lust for power and recognition are roots and, if they are not dealt with, they can draw a person away into deception. To have knowledge that no one else has, or to be in a position to meet all your own needs, can both be wrong escape routes.

"It is unfair to say that women are more likely to be deceived. There have been just as many, if not more, men in deception, resulting in scandals over money and sex, etc. Many of the cults have been started by men. The fact that it was Eve who was deceived, not Adam, has been used since mediaeval times to give the man superiority, but all the more reason why we women should know the Scriptures. It's not good enough to pull a few texts out of context and build your life on them. Nor should we excuse ourselves from learning by letting the men take responsibility for our spiritual state. I like being cared for by my husband, but I know full well that I have to work out my own salvation, with fear and trembling. I know I shall have to give an account of myself, and how I have used my talents, to God one day; and I want a reward too!

"I have been saved from a lot of deception by listening to

the Holy Spirit. He has promised to lead us into all truth (John 16:13). We need to check out revelation with others who have their feet firmly on the ground and yet have an appreciation of the Word of God. Finding out what God is doing in our sphere of the Church, and in the country as a whole, and getting involved with it, will also help to keep us clear! If we feel something is wrong in our fellowship, it needs to be discussed with the leaders, or checked with other ministries. One other way of increasing our discernment is by praying in the Spirit, which can activate wisdom and discernment in us. As we dig down into our spirits and hear His voice, we can fight in spiritual warfare. We do not need to be deceived by Satan as we become spiritually minded.''

For many of us, what happened in the Garden of Eden will always have its unanswered questions. Yes, the woman was deceived, but what was the man doing? Was he just plain weak? Why did he take the fruit from Eve? Yes, the woman sinned by deception, but the man sinned with his eyes wide open and he knew exactly what he was doing!

Anne Townsend shares about the context within Scripture. ''In the whole issue of women being more open to deception than men I feel that the idea is nonsense and not even biblical. If you take Genesis and try and get some doctrine on this out of the early chapters, you are misquoting and twisting Scripture. I have read John Stott's book *Questions For Today's World*, and his exposition on this subject is superb. It is rubbish to state that women are more open to deception than men. The reverse may be true, some men may be more gullible than some women!''

Bren Robson believes that both Adam and Eve were deceived. ''If we look at the context of the story, I feel that Adam also refused responsibility as well as being deceived. He passed the buck to Eve. In it all, at least Eve accepted responsibility for the fact that she was deluded. Having thought about this issue in depth, I feel that a woman is not more deceived than a man in given situations.

''Deception comes through the weak areas in our lives. For

me it has helped to be able to understand the society in which
we live. We have a very mind- and male-dominated culture.
Feelings have often been denied, whereas we find maturity
when our minds and our hearts are working together. Men
more than women have suppressed their emotions, and it
is after all from the overflow of the heart that the mouth
speaks. Having suppressed many negative feelings, men
often act from these and other prejudices and difficulties,
rather than from a balanced reasoned position. It is, I suspect,
for these reasons that most of the deceptions and cults have
been started by men.''

Eileen Vincent feels that the whole subject of women being
more open to deception than men has been blown up out
of all proportion. She comments, ''There is another fact which
is so often overlooked, and that is that there are far more
women worldwide in the Church than men. Surely the
greatest deception is that people do not recognise the Lord
of life. It appears to me that more women than men do! They
get free from the binding of their minds more frequently,
while men are more prone to pride and stubbornness!

''Many good Bible scholars have come up with very
different ideas about Eve being deceived. Women have
certain weaknesses which men do not have. Emotionally,
because of their biological cycle, they are more up and down
and therefore not such stable emotional characters as men.
But often, in times of major crisis, it has been the woman who
has pulled many a family through. If we just took the facts
and figures of broken families, in this nation alone, in the
majority of cases women hold the family together when the
husband has gone. Therefore, in that respect, it cannot be
said that women are weaker!''

Some of us used to accept the theory that women were
more open to deception than men, in years gone by. In the
churches women often form two-thirds of the people. So, if
women are more ready to commit themselves to something
that is good, equally they may also sometimes be more ready
to commit themselves to something that is bad! Women, it
was argued, are more open to the possibility of hearing from

God than men, as men seem to come to the conclusion that they can hear from God more slowly than women do, and again there is the possibility that women will more easily hear the wrong voice! It is also possible to have false prophets and prophetesses.

However, any Christian who is not walking closely with the Lord can be deceived. If the woman was deceived first, it does not logically follow that all women will be deceived first, just as God having made man first does not mean that woman is second-rate! The fact that the woman was deceived first is not followed by the fact that, therefore, women are more open to deception than men! This is borne out in things like the cults where men as well as women have been deceived by male and female deceivers.

General Eva Burrows feels that women are more trusting than men and therefore can be more vulnerable. But this is not the only reason for their not often becoming leaders. She explains, ''It is not just a weakness, it is also a gift to be able to think the best of people. Women are more ready to be receptive to religion and God. People often say that the Church is full of women. I think that that is a compliment to our sex.

''I do not feel women are more open to deception than men. I think the reason they do not often become leaders is because administration and organisation belong much more to the male psyche. It is not the first thing in most women's lives, to get up and be the organiser. However, for us in the Salvation Army, we talk about our founders, both William Booth and his wife Catherine. She is considered to be a significant person in our foundations. While he was preaching to the working class crowds, she was preaching elsewhere and had greater impact on the intelligentsia, and the middle and upper classes.''

Anita Traynar adds her own interesting insight. ''For me, it is clearer to say there are certain personalities that are more open to deception. These personalities can be found either within men or within women. It is very wrong to feel that women are more likely to be deceived, because they are more prophetic, visionary, or intuitive. There are a lot of men like that around too! There are also many women who are not like that, who are more logical thinkers. So for me, the issue is about personality not sex, which is borne out by the fact that a couple of women have started sects and many more men have too.

"The people I am referring to in this are the more intuitive, or in Church terms, prophetic ones. If they are reading the Word of God, and they see something, then they run with it very fast. They don't always check out with the Bible teachers and pastors or other ministers what they are feeling. So they pick up some of the truth, and push it to an extreme. They are then in danger of moving into deception or becoming off balance. I think that sort of personality can be found in both sexes, and it is a wrong assumption of the men in the past to view women as the intuitive and prophetic type, who will easily get misled.

"One thing that does concern me for the Church at large, and some parts of the House Church stream too, is the lack of concrete, consistent Bible teaching over the years. There is that verse in the New Testament, that talks of the end days, where many of us will end up being deceived. In the past we have often said to people that they should listen to their own spirit. But now there are some pretty strong publications coming out that many of us could be tripped up with, if we are not strongly rooted and grounded in the Word of God. We must be able to distinguish truth from deception. It is one of my heart cries at present that God will give me a deeper understanding of the Word, so that I am not one of those who will be easily deceived."

Often an intuitive person receives revelation from the Lord, with all sorts of things that He has not revealed in Scripture. Therefore, it is so important to submit that gift to other people. In marriage, submitting the feelings of one partner to the thoughts of the other, means coming to a good decision with which to proceed. Likewise, in church fellowship it is important to submit our insights and feelings to one another. This brings valuable judgement into our lives. Being under authority in our churches is a place of safety from the enemy, who is always on the prowl in order to deceive.

Ruth Calver feels that the men who feel that deception is an issue with women, do not understand the female sex and their different make-up. She explains, ''Women tend to feel things more, and are more emotionally biased. As a result, men can feel that women are going to take things off the rails, when in fact men need women beside them to put a different light on things, and to have that sensitivity that so often comes from women. We need to be harnessed together, men and women working together; not just man and wife, but with the man saying what is going to happen, and the woman coming in with sensitivity and guidance.

''I find with Clive that he will have areas where he has great strengths, such as trusting the Lord for finance. I would tend to struggle and wonder how on earth we are going to make ends meet. I have different strengths. If we had an all-male Church, it would lack heart and feeling. I find an all-male committee does not get everything right; they don't always see the practical issues. If we had a totally female Church, it would not have a lot of character and strength and direction. All-female committees get caught up in other kinds of problems. So we need to chip away at each other and then we will find the will of the Lord for what we are going to do. We can all be open to deception, male and female. We all need to be open to the Lord.''

So much of the problem seems to boil down to the fact that many women are highly intuitive, and many men are logically minded, and both are often poles apart. But at the same time this does not mean that women are more open to deception, because men using their minds can still be deceived. A one-man leadership is as dangerous as a one-woman leadership. The safeguard in all this is for men and women to relate to each other and work together as a team, as God intended, so that the weaknesses of the one can be compensated for by the other's strengths. Outside of Christ men and women are deceived, but in Christ we are free to become who we are meant to be, both men and women together. This we must learn to do without fear, understanding that God intends us all to learn and grow.

Valerie Griffiths shares from Scripture, ''We are all fallen human beings, men and women, and we are all equally vulnerable. 1 Timothy 2:8-15 is a passage extremely difficult to expound, if it is to be in harmony with other teaching in Scripture. Titus 2:3-5 commands women to 'teach what is good', a phrase which is commonly equated with 'teaching the law' for Jews. They are to train young women and children. If women are so easily deceived, the last people they should teach are other gullible women and children!

''Moreover we know that in the New Testament they prophesied, and we know that apostles and prophets were very important in the Church. Bilezikian, in *Beyond Sex Roles*, suggests that to prevent women teaching or exercising authority over men, while allowing them to prophesy, is like 'prohibiting women in the military to accede to the lesser rank of captain, while allowing them to accede to the superior rank of colonel!' So, 1 Timothy 2:8-15 is a difficult Scripture, but it cannot be expounded in such a way that it conflicts with the rest of Scripture.

''Whatever the problems, the passage *is* about how women learn, and it is important for every woman to study 'to present [herself] to God as one approved, a workman who does not need to be ashamed, and who correctly handles the word of truth' (2 Timothy 2:15). When Timothy was commanded to pass on what he heard from Paul to 'faithful people who will be able to teach others also', he uses for 'people' the Greek word *anthropos*, 'mankind', which includes women. Scripture gives us no excuse whatsoever for dropping out, shelving our personal responsibility before God, and 'leaving everything to the men'. Women were told to proclaim the greatest message of all time, at the resurrection.''

Sally McClung does not believe that women are more open to deception than men. She comments, ''In fact I would lean almost the opposite way! Women often have an ability in discernment. I have seen so many situations where God has built an intuitiveness and discernment into a woman. Often they have been used to discern the wrong of a situation and have been able to communicate that with a man in charge, in order to help him be more able in his leadership.

"Personally, I have an ability, built into me, of discerning into a situation. It is something that has always been there, and I have seen the Lord expand and mature it as time has gone on. Many times I can walk into a situation and discern something is not right. Sometimes I am not immediately sure why, but I will say to Floyd that I feel something is wrong. As I get into it, the understanding will come. Often I have served Floyd in his leadership in using this ability. Many times he has not seen things that I have been able to see, and so I have been able to help him."

Myra Blyth thinks that women in very subtle ways are told that they don't understand, and as a result they are easily deceived! She comments, "It is a most patronising approach, but it is incredibly useful! Women as a result assume they understand less and so do not believe their own perceptions!"

Christine Noble agrees, "In my research on deception, I found that out of nineteen cults, only two were started by women! Women have been warped by the enemy down the centuries, and because of this they are not giving their contribution. They do not believe in themselves, so deception is springing up because women are not contributing. I say this because often it is a woman who, on hearing something for the first time, knows it does not sound or feel right. But then her husband persuades her, with his logic, that she has got it wrong.

"Genesis is true in that the woman was deceived and the woman admitted it. In fact, in Genesis, the woman proves she was not prone to deception because if that was the case, she would not know she was being deceived. The deception issue has been used as a weapon against women in general, to push them to a point where their contribution to the Church of Jesus Christ has hardly been in evidence at all down the centuries."

What conclusions can we draw then from our discussions? Are women really more gullible than men? Eve was not 'totally' deceived, because she *knew* she had been deceived. People who are totally deceived are blinkered to see only their own 'truth'. Perhaps the main reason for Paul requiring the women of his day to learn in silence and grow to maturity was in order not to be deceived. He realised that God had created them like men with a similar capacity to learn.

The issue of deception has been used down the years to keep women quiet and 'in place'. Men know what the cunning of a woman can be and are afraid of being unable to handle it. Deviousness is difficult to 'get a handle on', so it's better to have a philosophy to avoid it! However, men too are as able as women to manipulate. Their way tends to be to use logical words and male dominance as tools! There is a clear link between "mere talkers" and "deceivers" in Titus 1:10.

As a result of this attitude concerning the deception of women, their sharing of dominion, having input, using their far-sightedness and their teaching ability, have all been reduced to a fragment of what God intended. Tradition, culture, prejudice and chauvinism have locked women out from shared responsibility within the Church, when the real issue and need for us is in fact to keep *Satan* out! It is ironic that the very tool, the gift of intuition and insight, which so often unmasks Satan, has effectively been taken out of the hands of the Church. Time and again it would have saved us from heartache and failure.

So restoration is necessary. Men in the kingdom of God need to stop blaming 'Eve' for their loss of Paradise, and recognise their own part in the disobedience within the Garden of Eden. Eve admitted her responsibility to God. Men must stop 'passing the buck'! Women need to reject their wrong reactions of fear or 'feminism', asking God to help them develop their unique gifts. We need to see that the root issue is not men as against women, but rather that only as men and women together will we see the kingdom of God come in, where there will be no male nor female. Somehow by the grace of God, we need to begin to move towards all that this means.

God requires of us all to love and to care for each other, in the same way that Jesus did, to the point of laying down our lives. This will only come about as mutual submission is outworked, under the Lordship of the Holy Spirit, and as we all recognise the gifts God has planted in us all. One of the gifts most needed now is the one that recognises the enemy at work.

For two thousand years that enemy has been able to lock up many with that gift. It is so often resident in the intuitive personality, which so many women have. As this gift is released to us, I believe we will see less deception in the Church, not more, as the enemy begins to be consistently routed. Then we will begin to work towards God's heart desire that men and women together will have dominion in the earth, as He purposed in the Garden of Eden.

Five

Intuition and Inferiority

The dictionary definition of 'intuition' says that it is "the immediate apprehension of something without the intervention of any reasoning process". It is the giving of direct and immediate insight. This is the mysterious aspect of the feminine character that can make many a man's hair curl!

Women, and some men too, often have 'a feeling' about things. It is not unknown for a woman to meet a man and 'know' that she will one day marry him! Within marriage, if the woman is fairly intuitive, this can sometimes be infuriating to the man in a given situation and so the logical debate begins. That debate often ends up with the man saying, "Why?" and the woman replying, "I don't know!" So the intuitive gift of the woman somehow seems inferior to the more reasonable logic of the man.

Within a historical context, it is interesting to see how the Greeks started this trend. Socrates was charged with not believing in the gods recognised by the city he lived in. He rather chose to believe in 'other supernatural beings of his own invention'. He believed there was a spiritual side to life in an unseen world. Plato, his pupil, developed this thought. But when Aristotle, Plato's pupil, matured, he began to move radically away from their concepts of the supernatural.

Aristotle affirmed the purpose of psychology to be the exploration of nature, essence and the soul. However, unlike Plato, he did not see the soul as a spiritual entity. He classified life as growth, sensation, motion and thought. He removed the mystical and provided method alone for investigation of scientific matter, that method to be based on the senses.

Our Western philosophy is based on Aristotle's philosophy. Our education emphasises only the logical approach to life and sets standards which crush many. Our science and technology is based upon analytical deduction alone. No credence is given to the unseen facets of human nature and life. Physical strength and beauty too are seen as of primary importance, while often strength of character, sensitivity or ability are not so highly praised.

So today our culture believes only in the seen, material world and this total imbalance of perspective has led to man being viewed ultimately as a small speck of dust, just another animal or just a cog in the machine of time, with no sense of direction or purpose. Yet deep down inside, we know we are of more value than animals or machines.

Even so, men generally seem to prefer a cold logical world to live in. We are less likely to give a forum to the more sensitive, intuitive people, who can often signal ahead of time if the course we are taking is wrong. This is a noisy world, where the best logical debater usually wins. Why are we all shouting? Is it because no one is really listening, or wanting to listen? Do we think that the sensitive, intuitive person, who might be short on charisma, is really second class, and thus, being 'inferior', is not worthy of our serious attention?

There are also those who enjoy the mysterious and go overboard into a world of feelings. They do not have the wisdom to see that a balance is needed. They can often end up moving into areas of the supernatural forbidden in the Scriptures. Just as Satan is able to hide within cold humanistic logic, and deceive us with endless argument, so too he is able to make use of an intuitive gift to his own ends, if it is not submitted to the lordship of Jesus Christ.

Within Scripture we have many examples of people who have flashes of insight because their intuition is submitted to God. They are the prophetic people. One example is found in Acts 21, where Agabus binds the hands and feet of Paul as he is on his way to Jerusalem. This is an indication of what the Jews will do to Paul when he arrives. Paul is then able to make a clear choice about whether to continue to go or not.

Today the Church is as much as ever in need of this gift.

Families need adults with insight. The Church needs every gift that God has given us. How are we to recover the use of this God-given gift? And why do feelings of inferiority so often accompany it? How are we to overcome these feelings in practice, so that the Holy Spirit can use our gifts for the benefit of the Body of Christ today?

Sally McClung knows that insecurity and low self-esteem are certainly big problems for both women and men. She feels that a factor is the changing role of women in society. "I teach about this and have done a lot of reading on it. Insecurity is listed as the No. 1 problem among women, and it often leads to depression. I have struggled personally too, in my own life, with insecurity. Over the years I have grown through this, and have seen God show me areas in my life and character that needed to be worked on, in order to bring a proper foundational security to me. I have needed to come to a proper place of loving myself and knowing who I am in Him.

"Some of this started when we were working in Afghanistan with the hippies of that time. I was sure God had made a mistake! I could not see how two straight, conservative individuals such as Floyd and I could be called to work there. Floyd adapted very easily. He grew his hair long and wore eastern clothes. It was much harder for me. We would joke when I put on my eastern clothes. They were always washed and ironed, which made them stand out! I just could not see where I fitted and where I belonged. The pressure of that brought out some deep and hidden insecurities in my life, of which I was unaware. This was the beginning of a process which lasted several years. It was painful and difficult, but very good fruit came from it.

"The whole area of feeling that we are wrong, when men do not agree with us, is an important one. Some years ago, we were involved in a situation where there was a crisis in our ministry. Some people who were working with us were in disagreement with our style of leadership. They began to work to bring about change. I felt something was wrong and I thought I understood what the problem was. I went to Floyd who thought that I was crazy! I really thought that I had discerned into that situation, and that the Lord had put something on my heart.

"I was confused that he rejected it outright. I prayed some more, waited a while and then I went back to him. Again he disagreed with me. This also happened a third time. During this time, I was struggling personally with insecurity. I did not have a strong base of confidence and self-worth. As a result, I came to the conclusion that I must be wrong, that there must be something wrong with my relationship with the Lord and that if I was so wrong, then I was really missing out everywhere!

"As it turned out I was right! The situation exploded. We had a lot of problems to deal with and a lot of mess to clear up. When the air cleared and things settled down, it became obvious to both Floyd and me that I had been right all along. He apologised to me, and it was a real stepping stone in our relationship, marriage and ministry together. He came to a new place of understanding on how we were to complement one another. He was not to be the lone ranger charging off with all kinds of thoughts and ideas. God had placed us together as a team to help one another. There would be things that I would be able to see and understand, which he would not. God had placed me beside him, to be able to serve him and help him in his leadership and ministry.

"Finding out that I was right built up my confidence. It built up my sense of knowing that I had heard from the Lord and that I was valuable and did have something to give. I also realised that I had 'blown it' in that situation. I made a mistake by dropping it, instead of being responsible before God, who had put something in my heart. I should have kept going back to the Lord to get more understanding and to find out how to communicate it in a way that Floyd would receive it, understanding what I was thinking and feeling. So we both made mistakes, and it helped us to understand how God wanted to use us in working together in the future.

"Many times women have something from the Lord and they share it but it is not received. Then, because of that underlying base of insecurity and lack of confidence, they do not press on in God, into all that He would say to them, nor into all the ways that He would use them. We must walk

through the learning processes and deal with insecurity in
our life. We will never be the women God wants us to be
if we are not building or rebuilding the right foundations of
self-confidence and self-worth into our life.''

Sometimes women are nervous in leading and almost
apologise that they are doing anything, as if it would be done
better if the men were doing it! We need to know that we
are called and we need time to practise and learn, in order
to take back the ground that the enemy has kept from us.
In doing this there is always a cost involved.

Grace Barnes shares how she was raised with low self-
esteem. ''Often I was told that I could not do anything, and
if I did I would always get it wrong! Going to a Pentecostal
church, where women had quite a lot to say and do, helped
a little. Norman too has always tried to lift me out of low self-
esteem. He has always listened to what I have had to say,
even if he has not understood it. He will then say to me to
hold on to what I feel for the time being. When pioneering
the church work, when Norman was away, I would have to
make decisions on the spot alone, and this too has helped
me develop.

''I do tend to pass things on very quickly to the next person,
because I always feel that someone else can do the thing better
than I can. I tend to be nervous in what I do, which is not
always a bad thing. It means that I can never do anything
in my own strength. There may still be a little insecurity in
me. People do not know what it costs me to be heading up
the retreats that we do for up to 1000 women at a time. I
would far rather be making the tea and supporting somebody
else, but God leads me on! I do feel that we need to be free
to make mistakes and get egg on our faces, if we are going
to move out at all. We must not be frightened about being
wrong. We must be open to people who come and tell us
when we have done it wrong too.''

Christine Noble has been able to overcome the attitude 'I
must be wrong' by verbalising what she feels and not keeping
quiet. ''Over the years I have told John my 'clunks' or checks

about situations and people. He would tell me how dreadful I was to think that way but then what I felt often happened six months or a year later.

"John now often asks how I feel about a situation with people or even, for example, in buying cars. If I say I do have a check about this and he buys the car anyway, the chances are that to discount my checks is to bring trouble on his head! Often the 'clunk' goes against the whole grain of what is happening and you would think I must be wrong. It is still worth verbalising it or getting it down on paper. You then have to live with the tension of waiting for the outcome. This is quite usual with most things of an intuitive or prophetic nature.

"I have learned to verbalise my 'clunks' and ask for help if they are too strong to handle. If it is in a public setting I ask for help from the men and women around me to put it in acceptable language for the situation. As a result, my 'clunks' are mostly received as being from God. It is hard finding the right time, place and method of sharing, or people who understand my gift. These feelings are definitely of use to the Body of Christ and often help to keep deception out, rather than allowing it in.

"I do encourage some women to develop their gift, by speaking and even writing down what they feel. Recording some word of warning or a prophecy which is difficult to receive will enable you to say, when it is later fulfilled, 'Do you remember, I wrote it down, here it is.' Moving in this way develops your gift, and when people around you see you sticking your neck out, they become more secure. Being wise after the event does not gain you credibility."

Men can often struggle with words like 'I feel' or 'something in me says', as they do not have that kind of feeling very often. Speaking carefully, often prefacing our reply with, "I can see your point of view, but to me it seems like this," helps our 'knowing' or intuitive feelings to be more easily received. It also helps to pray that the right question will be asked of us at the right time. Men who do not understand will question, not necessarily because we are wrong, but just because we are women! We need to learn to say what we feel in a godly way.

Patricia Higton's family happen to be of a dogmatic variety. She explains how God had to deal with her concepts in this area, and her ability to communicate the things that she felt God was saying to her as a woman with a prophetic gift. "Making pronouncements is a family trait, and the feeling that we must be right goes with it! This was very much in my own personality, but a lot of it was very fleshly. So I had to unlearn it. In fact, God had to bring me to a point of brokenness before Him, and now as I understand more what my ministry is, I can appreciate why He had to do it. I became very ill and after the illness developed a phobia about public speaking. I was totally unable to say very much at all in a public context. I can see now that God was allowing this to happen in order to teach me many things, such as humility and dependence on Him.

"It was during that time that I learned more about listening to God. I then had to overcome this hurdle, 'Can I actually hear from God, as opposed to coming up with something logical and rational and making pronouncements?' My evangelical background taught me you prayed about major things, and heard God through the Bible, the advice of others, and circumstances — and that was all!

"When we came into the experience of renewal we found that very young Christians in our church would begin to exercise the gifts of the Spirit far more readily than we did. Finally I just came to understand the teaching in Scripture that, 'My sheep hear my voice'. God had planned that all His children should hear Him. He is far more ready to speak to us than we are to listen to Him, and He must be very grieved that so many of His children do not really believe that He wants to speak to them.

"So I learned much more about His fatherhood, and came to a much greater confidence of being His daughter in a loving relationship with Him. The feelings of inferiority, to which women often succumb, are related to a lack of understanding of the fatherhood of God. Once we are able to have a right concept of God as Father, and somehow reach that position of faith where we actually realise He is longing to give us so much in the spiritual realm, we learn a new confidence.''

Eileen Vincent says that she too feels we need to train ourselves as women in hearing the Holy Spirit, which is more than just intuition. ''Some women do have a sensitivity of spirit, knowing what is right and wrong. Most godly men would recognise that and value their wife's opinion. In the Scripture Abraham is told to listen to his wife! Any sensible man of God will listen to his wife, if he trusts her as a godly woman.

''I have practised over the years to take note of first impressions. So often they are of God. In seeking guidance, it is unwise to adapt what you think the Lord has said, according to circumstances. You lose the thrust of what God is saying. The only thing you should do with the voice of the Lord is to obey it.

''Sometimes women feel that their most cherished good ideas or nuggets are ignored. This may well be true, but let them tell that to God. In a sense they are fellowshipping in the Lord's sufferings, because some of what God is consistently saying is being ignored by the Church, is it not? It is a good training ground, learning to control your tongue and emotions, and one which is designed in heaven and can produce fruit.

''A woman should not have an attitude of low self-esteem. I believe women need to brainwash themselves in who they are in Christ, being chosen, precious children of God and sons of God. Never call yourself a daughter of God because sons are inheritors and we are sons of God, just as the men are. We need to go against the spirit of the world, which would so squash women. Feminism too is aimed at squashing women, but from a different perspective. In times past, women were squashed by physical hard labour, and just by blatant cruelty. Today that would be outlawed here, so Satan has brought in the spirit of the age, to squash our minds and our own self-worth and self-esteem. Knowing who you are in Christ emancipates you.''

I have found that, of all the women I have spoken with, the major proportion of them believe that they usually sense first of all what God is saying. They hear Him say something is going to happen and then tell their husbands. We need to value what God is thus doing in our lives and not allow ourselves the luxury of feeling inferior. Inferiority is as ungodly as superiority. It is actually being irresponsible for much of the time. We must learn to build new thought and behaviour patterns. It is not easy to be responsible when we have learned to be reliant. It is easy to succumb once more to fear and inferiority and to want to put the responsibility on to someone else, getting them to say and do things for you!

Sue Barnett does not have a negative feeling about her own intuition. She explains, "I am a very positive person, which I have not contrived to be. God made me that way and I am thankful. So I don't necessarily think I must be wrong in situations; rather I am not afraid to be wrong, and that is something I have learned.

"It has always been my experience that the men around me have listened to what I have said, and because I have always been able to talk through my initial reaction, and have not looked upon it as, 'It's got to be right' or 'It's got to be wrong', I have been able to put into words and discharge what I feel straightaway to those around me. I have done this without feeling it was necessarily going to be accepted or rejected. Neither have I felt that it *should* be accepted. Rather it is all part of an ongoing opinion, an impression or a judgement.

"I have also learned from being wrong. For example, in team work I am not afraid to set the ball rolling in discussion with an opinion that needs challenging. I can, however, see how women can feel negative, because men cannot understand our initial feelings which are not always logical.

"I am very thankful for my husband's logic, and he says that my intuitions have been good. He has publicly admitted that he sets a lot of store on a woman's intuition. It may make him mad, but when checked through, first intuitive feelings about situations or people are very often correct. So it is essential that they are verbalised without the person who is giving them feeling threatened. They need to be discussed and debated without being bottled up. Then we can reach a mutual conclusion.

"But I'm not always intuitive. We don't have it cut and dried. If Doug asks me why I feel a certain way, I have to say that I don't know why, and that we will just have to wait and see! I don't make him make any decision at that stage, and as we also debate the issue this helps too.

"It is good also to find out what men's intuitions are. I like to get them to share, without feeling threatened about being wrong. Men do often have a first idea but think they must not act on it, as they must be logical and think it through! We must not be afraid of making mistakes. Even in leadership you become a very distant, cold leader if you never make a mistake. I want a team around me who are weak vessels, who may make mistakes, but through whom God is going to be the strength amongst us. Not that we set out deliberately to make mistakes, but I find that the possibility draws me much closer into a team. The people we are trying to reach all make mistakes too.

"We often try to be someone else, better gifted or more capable. God just wants us to be ourselves. As soon as we lose our desperate striving to be someone else and accept that God wants us as we are, then He can help us reach our full potential, making us comfortable with ourselves and others."

Just as men need to develop their intuition, women need the balance of logic. Women need to be careful about their intuition and test it. They need to listen to what the men around them are saying, to their logic and reasoning and objections, as well as to what the Holy Spirit is saying in their hearts. Women need to think and not be undisciplined. Women generally think as a whole, without all the logical steps of an analytical man. This is an equally valid way of thinking. It used to be considered a weakness, but is now being seen as a strength in such fields as relationships, where the need is to see whole situations.

Rosemary Andrews believes women have so many complexes about sexuality that they sometimes feel inadequate, inferior and worthless. She comments, "We stifle the flow of the Holy Spirit through us if we think we might step over the line, and teach or preach by mistake! When you have a genuine desire to serve and be used, anointing can be on you to teach, preach or prophesy and you should do so. In many places, however, this is frowned upon. We women have put ourselves down through the years with inherited fears and wrong beliefs.

"I know that when I was filled with the Spirit, I began to prophesy. Then I preached and taught a little, not because I was rebellious or desired to be seen, but because the new life in me had to find expression. Later I became conscious of my unfortunate position as a woman, and read many books on the male/female differences, their ways of functioning in the Church and how it should be done! I digressed into my former timid self, putting on false humility, which often ended in frustration. Feeling this was right, I endeavoured to be what I thought God wanted me to be.

"In my own home I was praying for the sick, teaching new converts, exercising words of knowledge and discernment, but outside I was very careful how I behaved. I lost my desire to study or take initiative, as I thought that there was no point in doing so. I could get excited at what God showed to me, but I must never let anybody think it was me giving my husband my revelation, in order that he could preach it on Sunday! I was out of order and so was my thinking. Giving my viewpoint outside of the home was questionable too.

"Today, however, I know that we all have to disinherit the many hang-ups we carry into our Christian lives. Most people thrive on encouragement and value correction and on the whole women need a good dose of both, as most of them are not assertive or naturally confident. The Lord once said to me, 'Don't put all the responsibility onto your husband.' That surprised me, because I wanted to give him a place of honour. But too many men are overworked and stressed and if we give support and take some of the workload, we can be partners, working together, as heirs of the grace of life.

"I have overcome my fear of being wrong by knowing that I am in Christ, believing in the Holy Spirit in me, measuring what I've heard intuitively by the Word of God, and by checking things out with my husband and others. Being willing to be wrong and be corrected has made me realise, however, that I am very often right in what I feel. I have not always been able to speak it out, when in the company of older or wiser people or strong males. However, if what I felt was not seen to be true immediately, it was often seen to be true later on. As you exercise your gift you become stronger in it. Women's gifts just need to be developed within the existing framework and structure of the local Church.''

Jill Dann shares that her legal training actually sat a little on her intuition. ''As a girl, with no one but men around me at college, I had to grow up with a pretty thick skin! I had to have reasons, not feelings. My mind usually had reasons, and in fact, the Holy Spirit has had to work on my emotions. I feel I am more in touch with my intuition now than I have been in the past.

''I went to a girls' school, which helped me. If you go to a mixed school, in any society the boy is usually chairman and the girl is secretary, and so the models are set up. With no boys present, we had opportunities to experiment. Also, I was brought up in the war. My father had left school at fourteen. He had seen too many able young women without training lose their husbands in another war. He did not want that for his daughters, any more than for his son. So we were encouraged to choose careers and train. My parents' expectations helped me and were such that I did not have the insecurities or inadequacies that many have had.

''Parents often do not expect as much of their girls as they do of their sons. This is something that as Christians we need to watch. I do believe in equality of opportunity. I saw some of my friends not go on to further education, because there was not enough encouragement or money. It had to be the boy who got the training, because he had to be the breadwinner. In this area, I see what the feminists are saying. I don't believe that there are set patterns in the Bible, saying that the man has to be the breadwinner.

''We are all told to work, and who is to say which work is the most important? Is the work which brings in the most money the most important work? Some men are superb at parenting, more so than some women, and I say that in spite of my gut reaction, which does not like it when the woman is the breadwinner. But this must be worked out between the man and the woman concerned. I am glad for a younger generation of men and women coming up, making marriage a much more complete picture than it was when I was young.''

As one gets older and the more confidence one has in being loved by God, the more one stops minding about making a fool of oneself. The risk then becomes easier to take. If God has brought us to this point, using this gift of intuition, then we must repent of self-deprecating statements and begin to risk it.

Ruth Calver thinks that in the Church there is a very big problem of women feeling inferior and insecure. She shares, ''I know it is something I struggle with today. I still feel automatically that it must be me that is wrong. I am very grateful that, being married, Clive and I can pray these things through together. I know that Clive feels there are things that I can do, that I feel I cannot cope with. He will push me out, and I know he trusts and loves me. The result is that I often do things that I would never do if left to myself.

''If we women do feel strongly about a situation, we should discharge what we feel. If there is someone in the situation whom I trust and respect, I would go up to them afterwards and say, 'Why did you feel I was wrong?' I would not want to have a big fight in the situation, where it would cause division. Some issues you can take or leave; some you can have a real burden about. For me, the family is one of the key issues today. If issues come up on it, I will talk it through and then ask, 'If I am wrong, why?' or 'Will you pray with me over it?' Clive and I often pray over issues. Praying is a great equaliser.

''I know in the past that there have been times when I've been destroyed inside, when I have really felt that I had to say something. I remember giving a prophetic word in a church and it was such a struggle to give it. I fought against it but finally gave it, and the church turned right against both of us as a result. Clive has never been allowed near there since. Some people there were really challenged and spoken to through it all and we have had contact with them since.

"In that kind of situation there is no point going in and fighting the leaders. I could find security, rest and encouragement through praying with Clive and those few who responded. I had to overcome the feeling that I had messed up the whole meeting, made a fool of myself, thinking that I must have got it wrong. Knowing the struggles that had gone on, and having to face all sorts of rumours that were spread around that locality about us, I was glad that I had talked with Clive first, and that he told me to go ahead as I felt it so strongly."

In our worst moments, when people have ridiculed us or men have refused to work with us as women or even tried to remove us, then we need to know that God is there and that Christ has been there before. He knows the pain of isolation and we can, therefore, overcome because there is resurrection. We also need our partners and friends to balance our perspective. If we can talk and sometimes laugh at the problems, then the grace of God comes through to us from another part of our lives.

Pat Tomlinson knows that in the past she has totally lacked confidence. She describes her early Christian life. "After my time with my small children, I felt like a cabbage. I was frightened that if someone came to talk to me, I would not be able to put a sentence together. For a while, I had difficulty talking as I would be so nervous. I had really lost confidence, so I had to practise and develop it again. All through this period there were thoughts and feelings within me that made me pose questions about what we were doing. I never let go, and kept asking questions of people like Dave. There was life within me which was very squashed, and it came out a lot of the time in a bad attitude.

"My experience has been one where my instincts have often been proved to be right. I used to tell Dave what I felt about something, but because I could not make up a logical argument to back it up, he would 'poo-poo' it, and go ahead in what he thought. Later he would find out the hard way that I had been right. To me this just speaks about the fact that women are not necessarily deceived, and that feminine instinct and intuition is not such a bad thing after all. It does give logical men a problem, and they have to work it through. I have had to work on my logic to get things across! You can't just function on intuition; you have to communicate, without ruining what you have in your intuitive gift. I know I am an unusual mix of intuitive and logical thinking.

"Dave too has gone through a progression. Way back he would never listen to things I said, but I still had to say them. I used to think that if I said them, and then he realised it was right, he would perhaps listen more the next time around. That has in fact been the case. At first he would not even acknowledge that he had listened to what I had said! Gradually he would acknowledge that he had listened. Then things would come out when he was preaching, things that I had said to him, but with no credit to me for having said them. Finally he would slip in that I was the one who had said it! This was a confidence-builder for me, the fact that he now valued what I was bringing and saying. My confidence has been built up to the point where I can now say things for myself, in whatever context I am."

If you are doing a paid job for somebody, you are under direction and you get some guidance as to whether you are doing well or not. The money at the end of the day affirms that you have done something well. At home, the only person who can affirm you is your husband. If a husband appreciates a clean house, that is good, but many women do not find their worth in housework! Working at a job in a team means that one can more ably learn from and give to other people, and so gain confidence.

Somehow within the Church we must start to give this confidence back to women. They need affirming and telling that being the weaker vessel is only a physical attribute. If women lack teaching, training, learning and discipline in the Church, they are going to make a lot of mistakes. The Church must help them develop their gifts. God created male and female to serve Him together.

General Eva Burrows recognises that she has overcome

feeling inferior as a woman in her own life, in part because she is in the Salvation Army. She explains, "Women are more readily accepted, both in the work at local level and in our administration centre.

"Even in management today, there is a realisation that intuition, as well as factual background knowledge, has a place in decision-making. Recently I saw a very interesting article in a prestigious American management magazine. This said that some of the greatest male leaders are willing to go out on a limb with their intuitive feelings, in addition to knowing all the facts of the case. In these days of computerisation, when you can have all the facts on hand, there comes another point at which decision-making involves a certain intuitive knowledge. For the Christian leader, that is enhanced by prayer and seeking the Holy Spirit's flashes of insight.

"The world today is masculine in style, often with aggressive competition. This new emphasis on the feminine psyche whereby, for example, it is no longer a shame for a man to weep tears, as it used to be, is the beginning of an acceptance of the fact that the sensitive style does have a place. I dislike all this unisex business, because I think men and women have different psyches and we have much to contribute to each other. God said to Adam and Eve, 'You are both responsible for the world, and you both have gifts and abilities to share in this responsibility.'

"Women's ideas are beginning to be more readily accepted these days. It is beautiful, because it is not that we are forcing it on people. Men are coming to recognise the need. In the world, they are putting more women on their boards, not for the sake of having the legal or statutory woman. Rather they are beginning to appreciate that women can come in with an insight, which may be intuitive, and they are beginning to be prepared to look at it. So any woman who feels her idea is wrong needs to hear this. There are aspects in this new thinking coming through that are more a fulfilment of what Christ was revealing than some kind of new, modern, feminist pressure."

Anita Traynar concludes, realising that culture must come into play in this issue. She explains, "Often English women struggle to give their contribution, feeling inferior. In America, women seem to be much more free in their social life than over here. But I think things have been aggravated here by the men who have come from the background of thinking that a woman is more easily deceived, and also thinking that men are the main vehicle through whom God will move. So they do not come with a hearing heart.

"Intuitive women often find it very difficult to verbalise what it is they are feeling. So it gets lost in the communication, and this leads to frustration for the woman, because she feels that men do not hear her. It is not just a woman's problem; it is also that men need to learn how to deal with the prophetic, intuitive type of personality, whether it is in a woman or a man, who also often feels misunderstood by his peers.

"I don't have a problem with verbalising what I think. My frustration is not that I cannot make my voice heard. I feel I can communicate, but I have not always felt that it has been given the consideration that it might well have been given, if I had been a man. That is almost a passing thing now, although you do still find that attitude, when moving through the Church streams, particularly those not so used to dealing with women.

"If I have 'a clunk' or a 'check', I can verbalise all the negatives I feel and all the positives quite easily, but not everyone can do that. I do have a different kind of frustration when I am working in a team, and sharing something which is not taken as seriously as I would like. Men are often less quick to step in when given information or gut feelings about something by a woman.

"I felt in the early years that my opinion was not wanted or needed, and it did take a conscious decision on my part (as I am a bit of a rebel by nature), for example, to refuse to become a typical house-group leader's wife. I thought, 'People are going to hear what I think and feel whether they like it or not!' There was no way I was going to sit there like a 'pleb' any longer. So I have obviously had my knuckles rapped a lot! At times, what I have seen has been right, which in itself has been an encouragement, building up self-esteem.

This makes you more willing to go for it next time.

"Although our men are now very ready to listen to what we have to say, I do not yet feel they are coming to ask our opinion within the context of our Christian work. If we want to voice our opinion, it is well received and thought about, but there is still that slight gap for me, where they are not getting on the phone and saying, 'What do you think about this?' Not that we want that wrong *over*-inclusion of women, just because, for example, the woman is the wife of the leader and not a leader herself, if you see what I mean!"

In conclusion, what threads can we see running through these shared thoughts? Intuitive people often cause reaction; logical men and women often steer clear of what they do not understand. It is still not very acceptable to show feelings; they are not given a place. Our culture has moved into emotional isolation, which is rarely breached, except perhaps at the football match! We are not particularly trained to handle positive or negative feelings, but are only trained to handle things logically. Education almost always teaches us that feelings are a hindrance.

Yet how foolish this is. Men, if not feeling-orientated, can be full of aggression, and yet they are never taught the way through in handling their aggression. The result is that it spills over into male dominance, which squashes even more the intuitive feelers around them. A further result of that can be that others move into passivity, unable to cope and so take the line of least resistance. The status quo puts the logical first, and with it male dominance prevails, because the great majority of men are logically biased. We either say that the differences between men and women do not really matter and that men and women are only different in terms of physical biology, or we say that one is really better than the other, and live with the status quo.

The Bible speaks clearly against both these statements. Firstly, men and women are each uniquely different. Secondly, God's intention in the Garden of Eden was not to have male dominance and female inferiority. That was the result of sin. Together, men and women, who have laid down their wrong responses to each other, will be able to found a new society where God is pleased to dwell.

Feelings are not meant to rule over lives any more than cold logic should. They must, however, be verbalised and heard. We must stop shunning them as the Greeks taught us to do. Satan would love to have inferiority and insecurity mask feelings and the intuitive gift, because it is often these gifts which unmask him. Strong feelings at the right place and time are good. They reflect God's character. All feelings have a right and wrong expression. The Church must, therefore, take them into account, as God is restoring all things to us.

Women in the Church need to deal with their feelings of inferiority, seeking the Lord, until they find release. We also need to remember that in learning to use the gifts we have, we will be like a baby learning to walk, who falls over. The baby gets up again and keeps on going and trying until he or she makes it. We need this tenacity, not feelings of inferiority and self-pity, when beginning to walk in new gifts.

Men in the Church need to allow women the freedom to fail, before they are finally mature in their gifts. They need to recognise that gifts of God lie within the female psyche and room needs to be made for them to function. Men, who are often threatened by women who have more apparent gift and ability than they do, need to see that tradition and male insecurity have to have women under control, 'in a box' for safety. The usual stereotypes of women are mostly 'at home', usually 'in the kitchen' or 'in bed'. As a result, we have a whole mishmash of binding thoughts from which men and many women need release. Satan has bound English men and women with such thoughts as these:

"A woman's place is in the home."

"Big boys don't cry."

"Keep yourself to yourself, and you'll be OK."

"Religion is emotional, it's for the women and for the old."

"We must have a stiff upper lip."

"Women are easily deceived."

"She's thirty, I wonder why she's not married."

"Women need to submit!"

"Children need to be seen and not heard."

"Leadership is male."

"She is the best man we have got at the moment!"
"An Englishman's home is his castle."
That last statement is, in essence, almost opposite to the
Garden of Eden. It is the fortress mentality, with a wife put
in a chastity belt for the duration of the husband's time away.
Somehow, for me, this goes beyond male chauvinism, which
is often just a cover. Many men are afraid of finding out that
they are, after all, inferior to women in some areas, or only
just equally capable in others.

The consequences of all that this means in relation to self-
centredness, pride and the ability to be in control, in thought
patterns, speech and life style, are very far-reaching. Men
of God released from such tyranny will inevitably bring about
a great release to women of God. If men feel threatened then
they too need to seek God in their need, to see how it was
really meant to be back in the Garden of Eden. Then with
the Holy Spirit's help we can work to begin to see restoration.

SECTION 3

WHERE DO WE GO FROM HERE?

Six

Singleness

The dictionary definition of 'singleness' is "the unmarried, celibate or widowed state". Either female or male can be single. Throughout history, the single woman was cared for and protected by her father or close male relatives, until she was married. However, as we move through the twentieth century, this is no longer the case, as family life breaks down.

Today within our culture we seem to attach the hidden meaning of second-class status to single people, because our society is founded on marriage and family. At times, seeing a group of young men together, we can make wrong assumptions of homosexuality. Yet Jesus and His twelve disciples were a group of such men. Jesus was also single and as such, was able to make a statement about which we need to take note. It is possible to be both happy and fulfilled being single.

Paul positively encourages the single condition, for the sake of the kingdom. He sees it as liberating, and for obvious reasons. He himself found it enabled him to give his whole attention to the call of God on his life, without distraction. He felt that with Christ's return imminent, as he then thought, the gospel could be preached further and faster if people in the Church remained single without family ties.

In our generation, there are so many more single women on the mission field than men. Twenty-five years ago, the ratio seemed to be about one man to thirteen women. More recently, I heard the number one man to forty women mentioned. If there are so many more women to men pioneering, can we accept that God got all these callings wrong? We also need to ask questions about the impression we are giving to the world and also about the lack of response among men. Christianity is not a female religion and we need to resolve this issue, within the context of male and female ministry.

So what is the feeling today about such situations, and what are God's answers as we move to the end of the twentieth century? What does the Scripture mean, in 1 Corinthians 7:8, that it is better to be single than married? For those who are married now, do they think their lives would have been very much different if they had remained single and not chosen to marry? Do they feel they would have been in similar roles today, with particular reference to their positions in the Church and in leadership?

General Eva Burrows is single and leads two million Christians in the Salvation Army. She feels that Paul wrote the Corinthian letters at an early time in his ministry. "I agree with those who feel that Paul at this stage thought that the Lord was returning very soon, so he wanted entire devotion to the ministry. However, we see a development in his thinking in Ephesians 5, where he speaks about husbands and wives and is encouraging strong family life. This could well be ten years on in his thinking, after he wrote to Corinth.

"In Ephesians 5, the relationship between Christ and the Church is one of love and enrichment and this should be reflected in the relationship between man and wife. It was an ennobling view of a wife, for both Jews and Greeks. From this I feel that marriage is God's intended purpose for us in society. So I am not critical of girls in ministry who, in that crisis of choice between singleness and marriage, feel that they should marry.

"God, however, in His individual concern for us, calls some to live a celibate life. This requires dedication to God and it is also a gift of the Spirit. He provides the grace to do it. Personally, I have always enjoyed male company and I don't think I am celibate by nature. I would have enjoyed married life and a family. Marriage is a beautiful thing, but the gift of singleness is beautiful too.

"Part of my commitment, which I have accepted, is to be

single. I had boyfriends at university but, joining the Salvation Army where there are many opportunities for women, I realised that I might be called to a celibate life. It did not give me great distress, because in that generation, being a single woman in a profession was not uncommon. At certain points in my life, as when I was in Zimbabwe, there were not the men around whereby marriage could easily follow. When the opportunity for marriage did come, however, it would have meant giving up my ministry, which I felt I could not do.

"I have definitely been led by God to remain in the ministry, rather than be married. I do not regret it. I may not have children of my own, but I have many spiritual children and am part of a large family. In a way it is a great benefit to be a single person in leadership, in that you receive tremendous affection from the people around you. My husband, family and children are these people and I understand something of what must have come to Jesus, as people drew near to Him.

"For us in the Salvation Army, single women in leadership are not an issue. What is unusual is to have a woman at the top leading the whole Salvation Army world. At this administration level, there are far fewer women. So I hope my life can be an inspiration and encouragement to other women and if a woman moves into this level of leadership with her own femininity, then I think she will be surprised at how well she can cope."

Pat Cook knows that being single enables her to be single-minded for God. She shares from her experience, "I have chosen to stay single. I am not single because I think I can serve God better as a single person. I am convinced that a married couple can in actual fact serve God more effectively in many ways. People think I am single because I have not had the opportunity to get married, or because I am terribly spiritual! Basically, I am single because I have never found the right person that I felt God wanted me to marry, although I have had several offers. Marrying one of those, who offered me marriage, would have meant giving up what I felt God had called me to do.

"Spiritually speaking, I do not feel the single state is better than the married state. Singles just have a different set of problems, and it is what you do with those problems that counts. Paul's statement on it being better to be single is for me something of an enigma, because I feel God created men and women to get married. I even wonder whether Paul, if he was married, had some problems with his wife!"

Bren Robson also understands many of the problems of singleness. "Being single, I have noticed that for many marriage has become a status symbol, a sign of maturity, and yet the Bible refers to the single state as a 'preferable if possible way to live', honourable and normal. The Church needs to reorientate itself, because singleness is on the increase today, partly due to the high divorce rate, and also because of the increase of separations. Some people also opt for careers instead of marriage. With the advent of Aids, by the year 2000 there is likely to be an unprecedented proportion of single women, because if the medical profession is to be believed, there will be many premature deaths, mostly among men. We have already lost a lot of our menfolk in this century in two world wars.

"More than this, I think single people are going to have a significant part to play in the next move of God. One of the roles I see women playing is that of responsibility and leadership. If a woman has no husband at her side, it raises questions for all who meet her. It is only then that we will find out within the Church whether we are prejudiced or not, and whether or not there are hidden agendas. We will then see the problem revealed for what it is.

"Singles face many problems in their lives. Physical affection is now suspect, except perhaps within the family. This brings pressure to bear on the older singles who become isolated and never touched, losing the God-given gift of communicating love. They can be lonely with a low self-image and, fearing rejection, are in danger of becoming hard, as they struggle about the issue of finding a partner. In the world they are subject to harsh judgements, with people often asking the unspoken question, 'I wonder why they are not married?' The reason may well be rooted in past deep hurts, even from a violent father.

"The Church can be arid for singles. Apart from the odd singles evenings, and some training for marriage, there is little in church life that involves the person who is 'alone'. Many singles have a negative response to the word 'family', and their state is sometimes seen not only as a disadvantage for living, but also as a disqualification for leadership and ministry.

"Things get so stereotyped. Recently, I saw a brochure advertising a leaders' seminar for just 'leaders and their wives', not only excluding female leaders but single leaders as well, whether men or women. I have also been told by a lady in a church that 'We don't have many single women in our church, and of those who are left, well ... all the good ones have been taken'! Someone else said to me, 'Whatever is wrong with your church, there are so many single people in it'! One church I know sent their singles for a weekend with the young people while the marrieds met with the leadership.

"Sometimes we have strange traditions in the area of singleness. Some say a single woman should not be taken home by a married man, but it's OK for a married woman to be taken home by a married man! The thing is that most of the affairs that I know about are between married people! This kind of legislation may lead to bondage and can create great guilt. The suspicious glances of wives and husbands do more to damage singles than encourage them. Temptation will come to all of us, but openness about our 'unhealthy desires' to a few close friends brings the feelings into the light and usually stops their growth.

"As a single person in leadership, I feel God is saying that He wants to lift singleness out of the pit into which it has fallen. He does not want to downgrade marriage, rather to upgrade singleness. Miriam, Elijah, Elisha, Daniel, probably Paul, John the Baptist, Mary, Martha, Lazarus and Jesus Himself were all single! Principles do affect our practice. If we have a married couple, we should not necessarily assume that God is calling them to have their ministry together. If they have a ministry together, that is good, but they can also have separate ministries. In life men need relationships with women other than their wives, and women with men the same. There needs to be openness in this.

"God wants to restore choice to single people. The enemy has stolen that, and in particular this is true for older women who feel single by default. By this I mean those who in their heart feel they want to be married, but who for various reasons have not been able to be so. If we are being called to be single for the sake of the kingdom, we have a choice to make and God will give us what it takes to accept it. The key is to discover what God is really saying. I encourage singles to gather two or three friends to fast and pray and really hear the Lord. To be single is a gift and a calling as well as being married. Accepting where we are is crucial, for today some are single but who knows for how long, and today some are married but who knows for how long?"

Here we have three single ladies firmly established in leadership. All have good working relationships with members of both sexes and all enjoy being part of a team. There are other women in leadership who know that for various reasons they would not have become leaders there, had they remained single. They are aware that they would have become frustrated and possibly gone abroad alone, finding adventure in the mission field a solution to their problem.

Patricia Higton finds Paul's words on singleness difficult. She explains, "I can only think that Paul had such a passion about serving God, he just wanted everyone to be without hindrances and shackles. I don't feel he meant the married state was inferior. If I had not chosen to be married, it is difficult to imagine the circumstances that I would be in today.

"A lot of the work that I do, I have been enabled to do because of who my husband is. I am quite sure I would not have been given the freedom, if he had not been able to blaze the trail, as it were, saying to people, 'Look, here is my wife, and she has got something to say.' He feels it important to set me free for my ministry. Therefore, people who respect my husband listen to me. Without that platform, it would be much harder for my prophetic insights to be received. I would have had to fight a lot more battles.

"Had I not met Tony, I may well have ended up doing something for which I was less fitted, in order to find some sort of outlet for the calling God has given me. I don't feel I would have gone overseas on the mission field, because I regard Britain very much in that light. But I am sure I would have wanted to obey God's call to serve Him, had I been single.

"There are many single women who are leaders in the Church in some sphere or other, particularly on the mission field. God has sometimes had only women to choose from, because we are much better at responding. My personal view is that a woman can be in a leading position whether married or single, but not in overall leadership, unless it is a situation where a man is not to be found to fill that position.

"Yet within that I see many leading positions that single women can fill. For example, in our church we use them as house-group leaders. We feel they need someone to confide in, so we make sure that there is a married couple that each single person can relate to. Those who have to go it alone in pioneer situations, as on the mission field, must be helped by God in a special way."

Marriage encumbers, yet many women need it and would have a lot of emotional problems without it. Many know they are called to be married but it has nothing to do with being oversexed. For them, with husbands alongside, doors of opportunity have opened which might not otherwise have done so.

Marion White finds Paul's statement on singleness quite a hard saying, because she is so happily married. "At creation God intended us to be in families, otherwise He would not have made Adam to be with Eve. So we need to balance what Paul said about singleness with the rest of Scripture, otherwise it is out of context. If I had not been married, I would have pursued a career in teaching wholeheartedly. I did some teaching in inner London and would have continued to do so.

"I think it is harder today for single women. Married

women have extra status. This is one of the dreadful things
that happens within the Church. When you are the wife of
someone in leadership, it is often assumed that you are a
leader too, when in fact you are not. Or that you have certain
gifts because your husband has certain gifts. I can see many
single women just bulging with gifts and abilities that have
never really been given the opportunity to be exercised.

"Why is it that women have been allowed to go into
exceedingly dangerous situations alone to teach people, when
a lot of men feel that women are easily deceived? And yet
they have let the women loose on tribes of people who have
never heard about Jesus and allowed them that tremendous
responsibility. Then when they come home they have to fit
back into a church situation, being allowed to say a little bit
about what they are doing out there, but never really being
given the freedom here which they have known in the
Church overseas.

"The other thing that single as well as married women are
allowed to do is teach in Sunday School, where children are
most easily swayed. If women are so open to deception, why
is it that men have allowed us to be Sunday School teachers
for so long without picking up on it? Interestingly enough
Rob launched a project a few years ago at Spring Harvest
called Urban Action. He was quoting William Booth and said
he wanted godly-go-ahead daredevils to go out on the streets
of the inner cities of this nation to win young people. The
largest response he had was from the women.

"Watchman Nee learned much of what he knew from a
woman. But it was difficult and people did not like it. As a
result he and a group of other men, whom this woman was
teaching, so organised things that he would sit behind a
screen with the men! This was in order that it did not appear
as if she was teaching them! They went to the most amazing
lengths, and yet he admitted that the bulk of his teaching
came from a woman!"

Grace Barnes shares practically, "When you write a letter,
you only hear one side of the story, just as when you hear
a telephone conversation, you only hear what one person is
saying. If the one side is written down, it gives a different

slant to the actual conversation. Also, when writing letters you might be answering questions or writing to situations. I feel Paul is advising in different situations in his letters. For example, imagine if Paul had been writing to C.T. Studd, who left his wife for long periods of time to go out on the mission field. He might well have said it is better to be single than married in his situation! Paul also writes concerning another situation, saying that it is better to get married than burn. This verse on singleness must also refer both to men and women, because just as men burn for sex, so there are women who do too.

"I do not know what I would have done had I not been married. I feel more free now than I ever did when I was single. I am fully satisfied, married to Norman and giving my life to God each day. This is where God wants me, and I have no regrets at all. It is Norman who has encouraged me to move out. I have no problems with single women being in leadership, because God is both male and female, and no respecter of persons. I do not feel that God's heart is saying that because you are single, you cannot express your gifts and personality, and if that is in leadership and you have leadership qualities, you cannot be a leader!"

Some women know that they would still have been leaders, if they had not chosen marriage. They were in leadership before marriage, in church or in school, and some were even called to be missionaries as small children. Destiny would not have been any different or better or worse; life would just have had different priorities.

Sue Barnett remembers a day about ten years ago, when she said to her husband that if she had not been married to him, she would have been doing similar things, even if not a Christian! "Part of that statement came out of the hunger I had in feeling there must be more to the Christian life. At that time, ten years ago, I moved into a new experience of finding what the Holy Spirit could do in my life. God was also showing me in what area my gifts lay, whether single or married! As I was developing these gifts before I was married, I feel I would have been out there in these roles had

I not married. I received a calling that was over and above whether I was married or not, and teaching certainly played a part in that.

"I have several friends who are both single and leaders, and I see no reason why they should not be, especially as Paul appears to have been single himself. There should not be a problem for single women any more than single men in this area. We just need to be careful of the close encounters, such as in counselling, that leaders often find themselves in. We, in Saltmine, generally counsel in pairs and avoid, where possible, counselling the opposite sex.

"One major concern I have is to draw people together. I hate the fragmentation in our country, and the splits in our churches that cause such pain and isolation. I long to unite people and include everybody in, regardless of age, gift, denomination, sex and status. My role in leadership often unites people from all backgrounds and encourages teamwork. I love teamwork, and we all need to know our limitations within our spheres of work. Singles often have valid insights into married life, and widowed people have a wealth of experience that we can tap."

Sylvia Mary Alison sees that if one has a calling to a particular function, it is much easier to do it if one is able to be single-minded about it. She shares, "In terms of leadership, I imagine it is much easier for a Roman Catholic priest to get on with the job, because he has not got a wife and family. Or if an Anglican priest is working in a deprived area, he has the concern of his children being raised there, with their education problems. Often missionaries have to return to England for their children's senior education. Marriage is a high and difficult calling. It requires as much vocation as it does to be single. In these days of stress and the easy break-up of marriage, it is important to make it really work, and not everyone is called to do that.

"Had I not chosen to be married, I still feel I have the gift to lead and would have done much of the work that I have already done. I was called to work in prisons while still at school, at the age of seventeen. So I went to the London School of Economics and worked in a mental hospital to train myself to be equipped for my calling. Twice in my life I had to die to being married and be prepared to be single, if that was what God wanted. If I had been single, I am sure God would have given me a job to do. As far as leadership goes, I was head girl at school. This was a natural gift and, depending on how it is developed, the Lord is well able to take the natural and do something with it. Both the natural ability and the calling are essential.''

With hindsight, some folk today could have done well to consider Paul's note about remaining single with the work of God picking up apace! Historically, during the last two decades there has been much teaching on being married. For many this has helped to form them, and marriage has given them stability and encouragement to go forward. For others it became a pressure in life to find the right husband. They thought being married to the right man all-important, and that this would bring them into leadership.

However, we can be released as we see that leadership is a gift just as teaching is. Therefore our *raison d'etre* must be in Jesus and in His developing of our gift and character. We now see single women, both black and white, in house-group leadership in south London. Not initially thought of as single or married, or black or white, they are just the people developing the gift of leadership. These women need recognition by the Body of Christ. Women of God do not want recognition just because they have married the right husband!

Valerie Griffiths feels there are some advantages in being single and others in being married. ''Singles control their own time, they are free. You have to find your own niche before the Lord, as to what He wants you to do. It may not be permanent. You may just be called to be single for this present time.

''On the other hand, overseas it was sometimes easier for a married woman to get alongside married women, and children are a tremendous help in making friends. I had openings in Japan, which Mike's secretary envied, but I did not have the time to develop them into leadership training as I still had toddlers at home. She had the time, but as a single person she did not have the contacts. So there were opportunities and drawbacks on both sides.

"A survey for the EMA was recently undertaken by Gillian College on *Single Women on the Mission Field*. They had the advantage of time and freedom, their sex and single status helped in the work they were doing, and they were free to travel. Women overseas were often less threatening than men to national pastors, and they were accepted by timid tribal people, who were afraid of foreign men.

"Difficulties occurred when the single women were leading men in a male-dominated society. It is hard for them, particularly in Islamic countries. They find it hard to lead a church, to teach and bring men into discipleship; they find church planting and pioneering hard (but then so do men), they find it hard to counsel married couples, and they find it hard working alone. But many of these problems are common to other missionaries too, and when there is work to be done, they all get on and do it.

"In the Far East, many single women are involved in evangelism, starting new churches in areas and towns where there are none. Others are training national leaders, Sunday School teachers, Bible College students, etc. They work in pairs, and are free to do everything men do in similar situations. I have seen men and women working well together in partnership overseas, and it makes the hang-ups, prejudice and fear that spoil relationships in this country all the more grievous. The Lord is certainly using women to build the Church overseas.

"The Christian handbook published by Marc Europe lists all British missionary societies, and women make up 60% of their membership on average. Some explain this large proportion by blaming men for their unwillingness to go overseas. But maybe the Lord chooses to work this way. What prevents Him from doing the same here in England?"

Anne Townsend feels the whole issue of singleness needs to be taken in context. She continues, "Paul is writing about his expectations, with the end of the world imminent. Therefore the job of Christians is to get on and proclaim the gospel! If I had not been married, because I have a good brain, I would have expected to climb the 'medical tree', and to take a leading role as a Christian in medicine here in Britain, or overseas. But that is easy for me, because I have a professional training. I would never have thought of myself as a writer! I might well have gone onto the mission field abroad. It is easier in many ways to go out as a single person.

''The problem with having lots of single women on the mission field is that it gives the nationals a peculiar view of Christianity, as a foreign religion for women, which is not led by married couples and doesn't have families in it! For young churches to grow, they need families that they can model themselves on. The ideal must be for married couples to be working overseas. This is not to the detriment of single women. My husband feels ashamed of his own sex, in that Christian men have left women in isolated tribal areas, sometimes alone, or just two together. It breaks his heart that men are not responding to what he believes God is telling them to do. He would say that men in Britain are caught up in a materialistic society, and are not listening to God.''

Concerning singleness and marriage, we need to understand that the kingdom has come, but also has yet to come. In kingdom terms there is no male or female or giving in marriage. However, in the present, when our personality and gifting are taken into account, some of us are gifted to be married and some to be single. A wife therefore can be anything in the Church which her husband releases her to be, and he can be anything in the Church that she releases him to be. These boundaries produce the continual need for referral and deferral.

Jill Dann knows that for Paul anything that took your mind off doing God's will was not helpful. She shares from her interesting perspective. ''Personally I did not want to be married! I was not looking for marriage at all. I had in front of me a very promising career. I was pioneering a new field. God brought me face to face with the man who was to be my husband. We met while I was cooking at a boys' camp where he was an officer! We had a year together at Oxford and got engaged. Then I did my final year.

"I never had to face up to singleness, rather I had to face up to marriage! I was married at twenty-two. I have seen the issue of singleness much more clearly since my two daughters have grown up. My younger daughter was married before my older daughter was engaged, who at that stage looked as though she was going to be single. I could see her problems with a younger sister getting married, and she not knowing what her future was going to be, yet with a career well and truly in front of her. However, she is now supporting her husband through theological college training.

"I believe I would have been just as happy single as married. If His best for me was to be single, He would have given me the ability to cope with it. He probably knew I could not cope with it, so He gave me something better, which was a husband! I don't know that I would have ended up on the mission field. I might well have ended up in politics, but I cannot be sure. I am very happy with single women in leadership. It is a question of gift and ability and God's choice, and that is what matters."

Jean Darnall feels Paul was talking about singleness in the New Testament in relationship to ministry, and perhaps particularly to young men who may have had strong passions and could be vulnerable to temptations. She continues, "On the one hand, if they could not restrain their passions they had better marry. Paul, however, as a married man himself, seemed to have a preference. He must have been married to belong to the Sanhedrin, as it was a rule that to belong you had to be married. But we don't know what happened in his marriage. His wife was either incognito or separated from him or dead, and we hear that his personal preference was for singleness, because of his complete devotion to the Lord Jesus and the hard life he lived on the road. His phrase, 'This one thing I do ...' was his whole attitude in life. It was not that he made a rule.

"If I had not chosen to be married, I feel that I would have been in a similar ministry today. This is because I was a woman in ministry before I was married. I have been preaching since I was sixteen years old. I was preaching at home and in other states until I went to Bible College. Elmer, my husband, had already graduated and had an established ministry before he met me. So it was really two ministries coming together recognising each other. We wore a double harness from the beginning.

"I think I would have gone into leadership if I had not been married, because I had favourable circumstances for it. I was in a denomination that recognised women's ministries, the Four Square Gospel Church, which was founded by a woman, Aimée Semple McPherson. She had a powerful, worldwide ministry, before she built Angelus Temple and founded the Bible College in Los Angeles under the name of the International Church of the Four Square Gospel. So there was a strong female image there and a model who was highly respected and loved as a very gracious and tender person, as well as being very gifted. In our college, people were encouraged to attend as couples and train and study together, and they were ordained together. So I would have had a place within my own denomination.

"It is very difficult for single women in leadership today, because they are more vulnerable to gossip and loneliness. If they work with another woman there are often problems of jealousy, or misunderstanding by people concerning the closeness of the relationship. So many accusations can come that they have to walk a careful path.

"We have noticed in our denomination, that where we have a lot of single women who have gone out and pioneered churches they usually surround themselves with very strong men, and they delegate more authority than the average man does. In Scripture where it talks about 'let not a woman usurp authority', the key word is 'usurp'. If the authority is a God-given authority, recognised by man and Church, it is not usurped. They are to use it well, as it is really stewardship. If they don't have that recognition and they are rather pushy, then they are out of place. That would be true for a man too. Paul, as he was writing, must have thought how little authority women had, or how little they were allowed, and if they pushed and usurped it, against all the cultural patterns of his time, they would be in trouble."

So, concluding our thoughts on singleness, we can see that many of these ladies know that they would have been doing similar things today, even if they were single. Their training would have been outworked. Others amongst them would have struggled as singles, as they recognise that marriage has opened doors for them. All women whether single or married need the freedom to follow God's call on their lives. They need freedom within the Church, rather than consistently having to leave the Church for the mission field or para-Church to find fulfilment and outlet for their gifts. Within the Church team all gifts can be developed, including leadership gifts, if the Church is willing, amongst both singles and marrieds.

It is obviously an asset in any church to have individuals called to be single, able to move out easily into what God is calling them to do. Many of our attitudes in the Church need to change. We will no longer ask how long it will be before a friend will be married, without considering if he or she may have the gift of singleness in their life. We must stop hurting our single friends by assuming there is something wrong with them if they are not married.

We need to remember the struggle single girls often have to make it as a person in their own right, without being able to hide behind a husband. A single man often has a battle against people thinking he might be a homosexual. All singles have to face the issue of life alone without natural children. For some this is making a choice they are able to make willingly; for others it is a battle to be fought through, because they are single only by default.

We also need to remember that we can relate to anyone of either sex, in every way except sexually. We can enjoy one another's intellect and feel affection for one another. Singles can have deep committed relationships and enjoy life. The only area forbidden is sex, which is reserved for the life-partnership of husband and wife. Somehow, within the Church, we need to recover the ground for singles to be able to demonstrate affectionate love cleanly, as John did with Jesus when he laid his head on Jesus' breast.

With the development of Aids there may well be a shortage of marriageable people. In one way, this will be similar to the time following the First World War, when many women realised there would not be enough men returning to this country for marriage. To have the issue of attitudes towards singleness resolved in the Church will, therefore, be an essential tool in our armoury.

God has work to be done, for which He will call single people. Singles are free to travel and can be a real unifying factor in Church life. For example, they can visit several homes in one evening. They must not just be used as convenient babysitters, just as marrieds should not be used as convenient meal-providers! Those who are married must encourage those who are single to be able to fulfil their call and, if necessary, stand aside and cheer them on. This does not mean that singles will be doing it all, but rather that together, marrieds and singles, men and women will be working to see His kingdom come.

Seven

Home versus Career

The issue of whether a wife and mother should remain at home or have a career has been a 'hot' issue in recent years and needs much careful thought. The issue runs deep. Men have traditionally thought of the woman as the person at home, looking after the children, and women with careers can be a threat to that stereotype. Today, other men are enjoying the extra financial rewards that a working wife can bring home, although most of them would not want to switch roles and stay at home while the wife goes out to work.

Women are re-evaluating their life-roles. Many are already well educated, and for them to be left at home means discontentment intellectually, even though they were biologically made to be bearers of children. For many of them it does not, however, logically follow that they should remain at home all of their lives.

Some of the more extreme suggestions recently made about planting human embryos in animals horrify many evangelical Christians, but extreme feminists see this as a possible release for women from both child-bearing and being bound to the home. Embryo research is opening up new questions, beyond even, "Can we reproduce without sperm altogether?" to, "Is it possible for men to carry an embryo after minor surgery?"

We see media films, produced in a male-dominated society, where sexual attractiveness is the main value of a woman. The result is that only a few women feel their image is good enough (the Barbie-doll syndrome). Many women today suffer acute inferiority concerning their image and roles. Home is a second-best place to be. We must fit the image, superwoman must have a career too!

Male and female writers have written much over the years about the need for a child to have a mother figure to relate to. They talk of deprivation if a child is unfortunate enough to suffer in this area. However, we see them writing little about the paternal deprivation which thousands of youngsters suffer when father moves out, leaving mother and children as a one-parent family.

Governments are male, and male ideology flows down from them. Most religions and professions are male-dominated, and Christianity has not been free from stereotyped thinking about women in their role in the Church and in society. The question being asked is, "What about the old stereotypes? Are they still valid?" What is the Holy Spirit saying today, through His people, concerning a woman's role at home or otherwise?

Ruth Calver begins by sharing from her personal experience. "I feel that each family or couple need to decide for themselves who is going to be the active partner in the relationship. In our situation, Clive is the one to be out and working. The job he is in demands a tremendous amount of time, so he is not at home that much. Essentially, my role is that of wife and mother. I feel that, if possible, I need to be able to meet my children from school. I try and fit everything else I do around our family life, as I'm out quite a lot in the evenings speaking or at meetings with Clive.

"I would dread getting to heaven to find lots of people there whom I have led to the Lord, but without any of my children. The Lord has given me opportunities, so that I am not always at home frustrated and bored. I have avenues of working that can fit in with the children, and that for us is the way we have worked this issue through. I think, when all the cards are on the table, the home has got to come first for both partners, even if it means cutting back on what you are doing, or cancelling the next two months' bookings! Often, as they get older, children need more time, not less.

"One day I trust that I will be out there with Clive, but in the meantime God has been good to me, and given me breaks away from the children. I feel this whole issue goes back to the issue of, 'It's better to be single than married.' If I did not have my four children I would be a lot more free, but God has given them to me and they need to be cared for.

"What concerns me today with so many Christian couples is that both the husband and wife are out working to the fullest extent. As a result the families are suffering. The children of people in Christian work have a lot of pressures on them. My heart grieves when I see women throwing themselves into the Church and its activities, out nearly every night. The children are left with one young person one night, and someone else another night. There is no continuity and they are not getting spiritually fed.

"We have been affected by the feminist issue, in that women are craving to get out of the home. But for me my family must be very near the top of my list of priorities. Today the family is under threat. We personally live under a left-wing council, who are advocating that homosexual couples should be able to adopt. But unless we are promoting a God-given life style within our homes, all our words sound empty. I fint it hard seeing children not being picked up from school, hanging around the playground, neglected, or children never having a parent at prize-giving, or open evening, or the school concert. Our time with our children is very short. We need to create a home that is normal, with fun, laughter, love and excitement."

Marriage is not just a big romp in bed that you can do alongside a career. A home and children to care for are a first priority for married people. There is usually not the time to give to too many other activities, but there are exceptions. There is a great need to prioritise, otherwise the pressures become explosive. We must also be careful not to be judgmental in our attitudes towards people who make different decisions from our own.

Christine Noble knows the 'home versus career' issue is a 'hot potato'. She explains, "The home is constantly under attack, the housewife is considered to be a second-class citizen if she finds fulfilment in being at home. The question presupposes that your home is not your career. There are lots

of square pegs in round holes and vice versa. If we go back
to our gifting in God, we must look at it within the confines
of who is at home and who is out at work.

"Traditionally women stay at home to spin and men go
out to work and dig and delve. Because of unemployment,
we are having to rethink our approach to structure in the
home. It may be the wife has the qualifications to get a job
while the man, who is without them, is unable to find
employment. People in the world are thinking radically over
this issue, and we in the Church need to do the same and
come to godly conclusions.

"The home should be a place of warmth, love and identity.
It must provide an environment where children can grow up
in security. It is better to decide before marriage whether you
intend to have children, as children are not essential and they
are a boundary. If you do decide to go ahead with a family
it will help to talk through your roles, rather than make
assumptions. One partner will, no doubt, have the main
concern for home-making and it is possible that it may not
be the wife.

"If neither of you have the desire to create that kind of
atmosphere and wish to pursue a God-given desire outside
of the home, then you will need to make sacrifices together
to create warmth and love for your children in other ways.
It could be right to have them cared for by someone else, even
for example a grandmother, who would enjoy creating that
environment. But that person would need to have the
family's interest at heart, so there should be no conflict.

"Childhood is a very fleeting thing and needs to be well
planned. Some women would lose their frustration if they
could see the timescale of their lives more from God's
perspective. They are creating the nest in which the children
can grow up and be used by God. This part will soon be over
and then they will be released to do other things. It will help
to lay down the 'home versus career' issue and hear what
God is saying in their whole life, otherwise it means there
is a fight all the time and nothing is a pleasure.

"If a woman's home becomes her whole life how does she
cope when the children leave! We must all be prepared for
our boundaries to change as our children grow up and as our

marriage relationships develop. When the children leave home and we have more time, hopefully we are more mature and able to serve God in new ways and situations.

"If your life has been totally locked up in your children, they have been not so much a boundary as a prison. We want our homes to be places where our children and also others can grow. It should be a training ground for us all. As I learn to deal with my children, so I am equipped to help others in their lives. If I am faithful in the small things, then God gives me more. So the home is never an end in itself, rather it is a launching pad into greater things and a wider ministry."

Jill Dann does not like the word 'housewife', because she does not consider that she is married to a house! She continues, "I am Tony's wife and a homemaker. Even among Christians, homemaking is undervalued. It is just as much a vocation as any career. But having said that I do realise that there are women who are single parents or just singles who have got to earn their living. Others actually need to work for themselves, even when money is not an issue. There are no hard-and-fast rules.

"I made a choice not to go back to my career. This was worked out through God's guidance and talking with my husband. I could have gone back, because I had training and now speak from that privileged position. When you have the opportunity to go back, it is easier to say 'No'. It is not irksome, because it is a free choice.

"I gave up my career and God gave me other opportunities. I was never stuck at home, although when the children were small we did not have a lot of machinery, so I had to do a lot of physical hard work. There is this difference between the older women and younger ones today. I have seen this difference myself with my two daughters, who are both now married. Each couple will need to work out for themselves how their needs will be met.

"I would hope, however, that people can be at home to meet their children from school, because this is often the key time in their lives when things come out, and you need to be talking. If you are not there you have missed it. I was very

fortunate on the days I was out, because the trains got me
back in time after meetings in London. I would be back at
4.02 p.m.! I was also fortunate to share with two other mums
in the picking up from school. We each took a week at a time,
and we would look after one another's children, and give
them tea if necessary, until Mum picked them up.

"God's seal was on all this for me. My heart was with my
children, and God also enabled me to do what He wanted,
which at times still seems like a full-time job. If you are doing
voluntary work, and if someone is ill, you can leave and
return home. If you are being paid it is much harder. I would
always ring home at 7.45 a.m., when I was away overnight.
This ensured that my husband was awake, the children were
up and the breakfast was on the way. If someone was ill, all
I had to do was get on a train and get back home. This made
me feel secure. My Christian friend, who was always there
as a back-up, also helped me greatly."

If a woman therefore feels that God is calling her to have
a career or ministry, then with mutual agreement the
husband and wife must work out how this is going to affect
the home, the children and their lives together. God's seal
will be on what is done, when we have asked Him concerning
our priorities.

Patricia Higton shares that if you have children, they
cannot be neglected without guilt. She shares something of
her personal difficulties, "I tend to feel that, if you can
possibly devote yourself to them for the first few years of their
lives, in terms of actually being around and being there, then
that is the ideal. I did not find it easy myself, being trained
to do something else, and then finding I had two children,
dirty nappies, and everything else. I also felt to some extent
that I vegetated in those years.

"In those early days, I had not learned about discovering
my gift and ministry, so I was not fulfilled in the Church.
We were in a more traditional church, and I was the curate's
wife running women's meetings, which I couldn't stand
going to: endless cookery demonstrations with notices and
epilogues! I thought I should be visiting people pastorally,

which is just not my gift at all. So there was a lot of unnecessary guilt attached to those years for me.

"Once your children are at school it is different. Any woman who thinks her home can take up all her time must have a wrong attitude to it these days! It is so different from years gone by, with so many gadgets, that you cannot spend all your time on housework unless you are totally besotted with your home! So if men feel that women should spend all their time at home, they are actually pushing women into something that is unhelpful, almost causing them to be house-proud. It is just not possible to find total fulfilment within four walls.

"We must be discovering all the time what God has called us to do in serving him full time. That is going to work out in different ways. For a short period of a woman's life, it may mean devoting more time to the children, then going on to discover and develop more of our gifts, both in the Church and for the world, which is essential."

Even singles need to learn the value of a good home life. You cannot be successful without a good home base. God created us with a need to have a home, and there is a need to work out the right balance between home and work. At leadership level, delegation of work is part of the answer to give more time at home. There is a psychology of home and relationship which goes deep to the roots of our humanity. We devalue it at our peril.

Myra Blyth feels that without a warm, secure environment at home, a career would be disastrous for her. She explains, "Home is the touch base which brings back meaning and sense and value. There are times in my career when I can be so excited, thinking we are about to change the world and nothing else matters. Equally there are such low points when I feel nothing is happening and I feel I am personally falling apart. It is then that I realise how important my marriage and home are.

"I love travelling, but I think it is because I know I have a home. If I had no home in terms of relationship to my husband, if I had no God, and if I had no physical womb to return to, then the gutsiness, grittiness and vulgarity of the working life would be more than I could bear. My relationship with my husband has kept me in my work. I would easily have ditched it, twice in the last five years.

"It has been interesting to watch a few friends who have been in the working world, and are strongly work-orientated. They said that once they had children they would continue working, but it hasn't happened, because they have gone through a change in the whole process. They are now fulfilled as mothers. There are others who are not fulfilled. The answer for them concerns me.

"Are the roles of work and family diametrically opposed, or is there a life style that enables a mother with children to work? There needs to be an encouragement from the Church for couples to have permission to experiment in roles. The social stigma of the man taking time off is encouraged by the Church. This is a mistake. Men as much as women need to be able to explore life to the full.

"There are other great experiments taking place where women are working from home, and that should be encouraged too, but not at the expense of the first experiment, which is more radical and the one that is usually dismissed. Women who do choose to go to work after having children should not be stigmatised as uncaring. Mothers and also others who choose to stay at home have not sold out the cause. We need more time in this area to try out new ideas, rather than come to rash conclusions about what is right and what is wrong."

For some, the feminist movement has gone too far by saying that a woman's self-fulfilment and career are more important than her role as a wife and mother. The reality is that they are both equally important at different seasons in life. If self-fulfilment or materialistic considerations predominate in a woman's life, this is a wrong idea of freedom. Very often children suffer as a result. Looking for ways to minister outside the home can involve children. As they get older there are more ways this can be developed. They have strengths in different areas and can complement our work together in exciting ways. True freedom, joy and liberty are only found in fulfilling God's agenda for our lives.

Sylvia Mary Alison shares how this subject of home or career has for her sometimes been a struggle in relation to her feelings of personal worth. "At times, I wanted a paid career because that is tied up with one's worth. If someone is prepared to pay you something it means they think you are worth paying. When my children went to boarding school, which we felt was necessary because we lived between Yorkshire and London, I then wanted a job. But I was hopelessly unemployable.

"It was at this point that the Lord said that I was not to take a job, as He had something for me to do. The next thing that happened was that I was asked to be on the Spree '73 committee and then to be Chairman of the Prayer Committee. Sometimes since then, I have felt that with all the work that I do, it would be good to be contributing to the family's finances, which I'm not doing. But home is a career, and very hard work, plus the fact that I have had several careers working from home. For example, Prison Fellowship work and the Parliamentary Wives group have both been done because I have been available.

"So for myself, I have really resolved the conflict of home versus career, as my careers have flowed out of my home life and wifehood. I would not say to anyone else that they ought to do what I have done. Many of my female relatives have had careers and raised families at the same time, but the Lord has called me to marriage, which is a picture of our relationship with Him. As He shows me a need here or there, and says, 'Can you help Me in this area?', He leads me to be responsive to His heart for prisoners and for people in positions of authority. His heart is to save those who are lost, and this is where He has led me to work. I now no longer feel a lack of worth because I am not paid, but my worth comes from knowing Christ's love for me."

Marion White says that she finds this one of the perennial issues, which for her has never been an issue! As she explains, from personal experience, "I have always been so happy and busy at home that I have not had time to think about pursuing a career, neither have I wanted to. But it is a very individual thing. I have heard people say that to be a good mother you have to stay at home and look after the family. I know to an extent there is a lot of truth in that, when the children are small.

"One of the real burdens on my heart at the moment, which I've been speaking about quite a bit, is that as women we should be 'mothers in God'. That doesn't just mean those who have children, but also single women and those without children. The fact is that we have a tremendous ability within us to mother people, and to care for them. Our society is desperately in need of women who can mother people, whether lonely people, or people who have been abused, or people who have not had good family relationships.

"I would say we need a lot more women as mothers, and that does not conflict with whether or not they have a career. There is a point in simply being at home and being available. At the same time I know a lot of good mothers who go out to work. Some of them have to, some choose to. They are nonetheless exceptionally good mothers and good wives. So it is a delicate issue, and you can stir up problems if you come down strongly on one side or the other.

"In Titus, Paul talks about older women teaching younger women. Sometimes I have seen a real lack of that in churches, because the older women have all gone back to work. There are also often younger women who have moved away from home when married, with small children, who long for someone motherly to show them what to do, or to help, or just to be there."

Women are able to put value on people's lives and nurture them because God has made them with a sharing capacity, not only in the procreation and preservation of the race, but in the cultural tasks of making a better society. Women, having a gift for compassion and personal relationships, have the capacity to draw men back from the computerised, dehumanising society of today by emphasising the value of people. Men are interested in destiny and in where they are going. Women are interested in the people that they meet on the way.

Anita Traynar shares that when she first came into the House Church, God was definitely restoring family life and families as the cornerstone of His kingdom. ''We had a lot of teaching and priority given to this, in such a manner that if you were single, you really did feel a second-class citizen. There was no hope for you until you got married. So, making a good home for the husband and being available for the kids was, at that time, priority, and it still should be. But I think if anyone was then considering a career, they would have felt quite a weight of spoken or unspoken opinion against them from the fellowship.

''That has changed now. For a woman it is a very fine line to walk, so that her calling into a career or into what God is doing does not detract from her calling as a wife and mother. For some, their home life is definitely enhanced by the fact that they have got outside interests and an outside calling. I know that I am the kind of personality who would get very bored with just a home to run. So although there have been different time pressures, particularly with my husband on the road as well, in full-time ministry, I still feel that moving out into my calling and having stimulating outside interests has enhanced my role as a wife and mother.

''I feel that God will not be quite so interested in what I have done for Him in education, as He will be in what I have done in Jonathan, Emma and James, my children. I always keep that before me. As a family, we have time booked into the diary which is very clearly family time, even if that cuts across church meetings. This is a high priority for us. We try to make at least one weekend a month, and preferably two, a family weekend where the children can choose what they do. Unless it is a dire emergency, neither of us would put appointments in at that time.

''Ian and I have to have time that is booked into the diary, which is as sacred as an elders' meeting would be, to be able to keep the communications going. Otherwise the pressures build up. I review my priorities each year and if something has to go, it has to go. You never seem to stick with just your workload — you always seem to gather more through the year.

''So the emphasis for us is changing from where women

did everything in the home, to where husbands are seeing the homes as a joint venture, which will release women. I recently heard of a couple in another fellowship, where the husband was positively encouraging his wife to get back into some work as a GP. This was refreshing and it was because he felt it was just as important for her to be fulfilled as it was for him.''

Some would never call themselves career women. They know only that they are called to be servants of God. Within this they feel that He would first have them not neglect their home. However, many women are bored when their children are older and it is good if they can put their excess time and energy into serving the Lord, within the framework of the Church. If women want to work or feel they need the money, asking ''Will my family be affected?'' places a good heart attitude at the centre of our motivation.

Anne Townsend is concerned about the early years of a child's life. ''If you are a woman with children, the norm is that your primary responsibility is towards your children, particularly during those first five years of their life, when they most need the influence of their mother. Of course there are exceptions to this. After that age I think much depends on how good you are at juggling things!

''If you are clever and can run your home in your sleep that's OK, but if you are a plodder and not very organised you are going to find it hard trying to do anything else. A great deal also depends on your husband. If you are going to have a dual career and family, then your husband must be prepared to do half the housework, and that does mean half the housework! It doesn't mean he does the hoovering, and she does everything else!

''I think in many Christian families today our materialistic expectations are too high. We want to buy things that God does not want us to have. Therefore the wife is under pressure to work, when perhaps God would rather she was at home simply being the centre of that family for a certain number of years. But I would not want to put any hard-and-fast rules to this.''

Some women do not believe this issue is an 'either/or' situation. For them it is possible to fulfil responsibilities in the home, caring for husband and children, *and* have a career or ministry outside the home. Choosing to be married has meant that husband and children have become priorities in terms of ministry and other things come behind them, and being fairly organised enables the combination of both home and ministry.

Valerie Griffiths has never thought of herself as a career wife, but in following the Lord's call she has never been able to devote herself just to her home. She reflects, "I could not live in a town with only a handful of Christians and close my door on everybody else. My responsibility to my neighbours, when we were in Asia, required hours spent daily on language study, for several years, while I was having children. So I have always been fitting things in around the children and still do.

"There have always been demands of language study, people wanting help with English, opportunities for evangelism and Bible study, etc. Partnership is the realistic basis for marriages in this situation. Husbands are often away travelling and a wife must take responsibility for home and children and any demands made by others in his absence. He, in his turn, often has to undertake family responsibilities, because of demands made on her, especially in the initial years of language learning.

"Living overseas also involved agonising decisions over the children's education. If they had returned to Britain with no English education at all they would have had massive problems. But the Lord had called us and He cared for them even more than we did. We had to follow Him and trust Him to provide for them. He did not fail us.

"One Christian college in Britain, which tells the wife that her husband is there to study and that she is there to see that he gets on with it, is falling far short of preparing couples to serve together. It is very short-sighted and raises major doctrinal questions on the personhood of men and women. In many cases Christian women are the only ones who can reach other women who comprise 50% of the world's population.

"Romans 16 reveals the extent to which women worked alongside men in the early Church to proclaim the gospel. A man is set free for his ministry through the practical support of his wife carrying the responsibilities of home and children. She can only be free for her ministry if he realistically faces his own responsibility to share in the home and set her free.

"Children must be a mother's first responsibility but not the only one. I think children need a mother around until they are sixteen. The twelve to fifteens should not be running wild without supervision. Is this why the crime rate amongst the lower teens is rising, with lack of parental input at this time? However, as they grow older, many women need to seek the Lord's will for their later years. Paid work is not the only option. The important thing is to know what God wants at each stage."

Jean Darnall remarks that the 'versus' in the question sounds a little competitive. "If a woman is called to ministry or called to do something in the world in a specific area, there needs to be a discussion and an agreement between her and her husband either before the marriage, or after, if it comes up later. Things like the amount of time taken up by it, the energy required, and the pros and cons really need to be considered. Obviously, as far as Christians go, it is a question of whether the Lord wants it and what necessary adjustments we have to make.

"I don't think I could have kept a home and a ministry as well as I have, which isn't perfectly, if Elmer and I had not agreed on a 50/50 situation. He helps me in the home as much as I help him in the ministry. We work together in the Church as well as in the home. There is no feeling of 'Well, that's your job and not mine!' It is *our* work together. The house is really part of the ministry. When we have pastored churches, we have always considered the house or parsonage as belonging to the congregation, in the sense that folk were as welcome to come there for ministry, as they were welcome to come to the church.

"I have always tried to have our children feel part of our ministry too. They are grown now, with their own families and all Christians too, praise the Lord. Recently, we had a family party and they said the thing they appreciated the most was that they never felt that they were a problem to us concerning the ministry. We never left them behind. We made our decisions together, and they were a part of it all.

"I used to worry about all the travelling we did, and the changes of school. I wondered if they would be misfits. But what worried me most was that they might grow up to hate the Lord and the Church and we prayed a lot about it. But they now realise how their lives have been enriched by all the people they have met and how adaptable they have become as a result of the changing situations. This has been God's grace to us, that they were grateful for being included, and not shut out from our ministry."

The phrase 'home versus career' implies conflict and tension, which can also be good. It means that we need to continually reassess priorities. When God shows you your priorities, it is not destructive. Time with children is a tremendous training ground. Ministry grows out of it. Men also have the need to be fulfilled at home as husbands, fathers and homemakers. Husbands and wives who are constantly open to God for new initiatives bring a freshness and excitement into the family home.

Pat Tomlinson shares that in her situation, this whole subject is still a developing one: "Since we came to London it became the norm that I would get up in the morning, rush round, put the washing into the machine, do a few jobs then come to the office. Then I would go home, cook a meal for up to eight people and clear away before going out in the evening to a meeting. This became too much, so we reduced the people living with us, and Dave began to take some responsibility with cooking.

"It started in the summer with Dave doing barbecues, and it progressed from there! I am really pleased, because it is a practical development of a woman's liberation. I mostly cook now when Dave is away, otherwise I expect him to do it. We also had a home help for a while, but now our youngest is going to take on helping in that area. So it is just a case of fitting in what needs doing, but it is no longer all up to me.

"This is not quite like a career. Rather as a family and a husband and wife we are in it together. It is just a matter of how you work it out with all the practicalities. Obviously the needs of our family have changed as our children are all fifteen-plus and not as demanding as younger children are. I do still sit down and talk regularly with them about it all, and they seem quite happy. They know that I will change what I am doing, should they need me to do so for a period of time, as I will always put them first.

"I was trained to teach although basically I did not want to be a teacher. My mother wanted me to go to university like my sister. She just never stopped working and I did not fancy that. So I compromised. I took further education without going to university. I did well and enjoyed the course, and I learned a lot. I also became a Christian and met Dave at college, so college certainly made me think a lot which was invaluable."

So in conclusion, we see that home and family are under threat and that we need to devote care and time to our children's lives. We also need to consider what it means when we find someone who is unfulfilled at home. Home is a good training ground but not an end in itself. We all have a role to play in the society in which we live. God wants us to move on in partnership with our husbands in developing our gifts and abilities.

We know that family life has changed through the centuries. There was a time when the whole family worked the land together to get their food. Gradually barter was replaced by money and someone had then to bring home money to buy food, and industrialisation came in. More men went to work all day, and women remained at home with children. This is now the accepted status quo, and men with no job feel a failure, whilst housewives often feel trapped at home.

The Bible speaks clearly on this issue. Firstly, God told Abraham that His name was El Shaddai. This means, "It is God who provides". Our God is the God who is enough (Genesis 17:1). We must take this to heart and see it as the basis of our existence. Knowing this means we can trust God for everything that we need. We are then free to be able to work out, within our families, what God is saying to us individually about earning our food. The New Testament helps us to see that this 'working out' must be on a right foundation. In 1 Corinthians 11:11 we are told that: "In the Lord ... woman is not independent of man, nor is man independent of woman. For as woman came from man, so also man is born of woman. But everything comes from God."

In the past we have talked about the father alone representing God to His family. This role model can bring out worry and fear in many, as it is a role model after an image of their own making, often from an unhappy personal history. God's image is something else altogether. Sometimes, in our homes, the stereotypes must be reset, if not done away with altogether. Fathers need to be showing not male weakness, nor male dominance over their children, but a right use of 'maleness'. Mothers need to be showing not female fear, nor female aggression, but a right use of femininity. It is only these two together that make up the whole image of God.

In the 'battle of the sexes', our children need to see how problems are resolved in relationships. They need to see love, respect and mutual submission. They need to see good judgements, not dominance or aggression. They must see Mum and Dad functioning together to understand fully what God is like. With that foundation they will be able to move into the world, as adults in their generation, with answers to the situations they find themselves in.

The Bible also speaks concerning the good wife. The well-known Proverbs 31 gives the qualities of a good wife. She works at home and outside the home. She has many qualities, to shame many women! However, when considering which qualities are most often mentioned, it can be seen that working and trading and earning money come high on the list. This lady is certainly not 'confined to barracks'. From a well-ordered home she moves out into the world.

Jesus talked about us using our talents wisely and letting them multiply and bear fruit. Looking at the career issue perhaps more in the light of a person's progress through life may aid our ability to understand what God has in mind for a man and a woman. There are times and seasons in a woman's life. Times of sacrifice and times of fulfilment. We are called to serve, not out of pressure to conform to an image, but out of love.

Marriage is not an occupation, it is a relationship. The marriage relationship does not occupy a couple's complete time, therefore God said in the Garden of Eden that they were to rule as well, or have occupation. We must have a correct view of marriage. Considering marriage as the main career for women devalues the state of the single woman. Attitudes need to change.

Men and women must together after prayer settle the issues within their marriage relationship. There should be no stereotypes in the kingdom of God. Every person is unique. Looking at each other's gifts, being able to lay down things for each other, each esteeming the other as higher than him- or herself, such attitudes as these will produce a marriage where the Holy Spirit is Lord.

With the breakdown of families and society and all that that means, if the Church reacts wrongly in trying to maintain the status quo with traditional roles, we may well miss what the Holy Spirit is now saying to the Church, and end up with another denomination, within a generation, of those who believe it is essential to maintain a hierarchical structure at all costs. John Noble has said that the New Testament has male pictures of the Church — the Body of Christ and an army, but there are female pictures too — a bride and a woman crowned with glory. I believe that God wants maleness and femaleness to come through to maturity. This starts in the home just as it did in Eden. As men and women seek God to know how they should live and function together, the result will be that God's kingdom will be built on the cornerstone of the home and family where the Holy Spirit is Lord.

Eight

Into the World?

Until this century women have tended to be at home. Theirs has been the local world of town or village. In this generation, the issue of concern for the wider world has come to the fore, particularly with the development of television and satellite communications. We could be torn in so many directions. We must be clear what God is saying to us, as individuals and as churches in our generation.

Half the world is female. In some countries it is essential for women to reach women, as custom would forbid men reaching out to women. Issues concerning women and children obviously need female input, as women are carers and by nature generally see the issues at stake fairly clearly. They tend to see the end from the beginning, and often want to cut through the red tape.

Those who are not so keen to see women involved in the social scene are those who feel that women should be at home, caring for their husbands and children. They feel that while the men are out 'earning the bread', if the women are out 'following causes' the children will suffer.

So what is the answer to this situation? What do leading women in the Church today feel about their role in relation to the social issues that face us in the world? What do they feel about social work amongst women in particular, in the areas of abused wives and children? As the Holy Spirit motivates us to be involved in social action, how are we to handle all that God is calling us to do? Some women are already moving out beyond home and are able to share with us how God is leading them.

Valerie Griffiths, returning to England after many year overseas, has some interesting insights concerning the insula situation that Christians often find themselves in. "It has been said that the more senior people become in the Church, the less contact they have with the non-Christian world. Too many Christians never meet non-Christians socially. When we returned to this country permanently, I found mysel living between college and church in entirely Christian circles I had to think through what I should be doing in the community in which I lived.

"At the same time family members were facing unemployment and I was appalled at some of the corruption and exploitation I found in British society. I finally joined the National Council of Women, a secular non-party group of women which co-ordinates many other women's groups working for the welfare of families, especially women and children. The council responds to parliamentary legislation and where appropriate makes recommendations at government level.

"I believe God cares for the world He has made, and it is part of Christian witness to be involved and speak up against injustice, standing for what is good and right. It is part of ministering to a broken world, and we need to be where the people are, standing alongside them, demonstrating in our lives that God cares about them. If Christians were really shining as lights in the world, I believe far more people would see the love of God demonstrated. Time and again the prophets called on the people of God to 'do justice', to see that right is done, and to protect the weak. God has no time for worship that ignores this (Amos 5:21-24).

"John Gladwin in his book *God's People in God's World* says:

'The call of Christian life is to live in the world in a way that is not of the world. It is never a call to escape being of the world by refusing to live in the world ... The lifestyle, concerns and values of Christian people and of the Christian Church are part of the testimony of Christ ... people who cut themselves off entirely cannot preach the gospel at all.' "

Jill Dann explains that she is actually a trustee of the Church of England Urban Fund, which was a new venture started in 1988. "We wanted £18m, so that we, with other Christians, can do something about our urban priority areas. We want to be able to spend £4m a year getting into those central city areas, where the Church of England still has some presence, and where many other Christians have left, and occasionally new sects have come in.

"I am interested also in housing and the media. I would like to see some women get involved with young people's magazines, where a lot of stereotypes are set. Our young Christian girls are picking up those magazines and swallowing the images as though they were the truth. Some of the pioneers against slavery in the last century were women. Harriet Beecher Stowe in America did amazing work, along with some other Christian women. Those women suffered terribly for what they did. Christians were in the forefront when it came to temperance questions, and prostitution. So I hope that women will be involved in these and other areas.

"There are so many areas to get involved in that we have not got enough women to go around! Some have gifts in their hands, just caring and loving these people. Others should be knocking on the doors of politicians, and writing to the papers. Here too, I do feel for those men who by character are gentle and sensitive and who are not enabled to use the gifts God has given them, because it is not expected that men will be like that in personality. People do not know what to do with them!

"I am thinking here particularly of people who are out of work or retiring early. Opportunities for those sorts of men are needed, so that perhaps for once their gifts can be valued. Jesus was involved in the service of mankind, physically and spiritually. He healed the sick, fed people, opposed injustice and inequality. For Him it was service all the way. This is what He requires of us too."

General Eva Burrows talks about the involvement of the Salvation Army in the world. "The Salvation Army is a vital spiritual force with an acute social conscience. We work in communities, with the old, with children and young people and with families in need. We are involved with the homeless, the destitute and finding missing persons.

"Being involved in areas of social concern related to women, we have found it good to involve not just women alone, but couples. For example, in our battered wives centres, there will be a husband and wife both working together. Earlier, the Salvation Army tended to have single women working with women. We have now changed a great deal, and are introducing more men into these situations.

"The reason for this is that we have found that a woman who is a battered wife is quite often helped by the fact that there is a man in the environment as well as a woman. Our social work for men used to be totally separate from our social work for women, but not now. They are joined together and men and women work in all sections."

Evangelical Christians are getting their social conscience back, and are realising that the nation has sunk so low partly because they have opted out. There is something very lacking in a ministry which does not have a heart for social justice, because social justice is very much in the heart of God. A 'para-church' has arisen sometimes because the local church has not been doing its job. We are told to transform the world, not to run away from it. Over-concern with the internal life of the Church is actually so clubby that it creates another world, which has very little to offer those who do not choose to join the club!

Anita Traynar knows that the Church must now become more involved in social concerns. From her past experience in the House Church stream, she remembers, "We have had a couple of decades where we have enjoyed God, with our lives having been sorted out to a certain extent, yet I feel that for some of us, we are playing at Church because we are not sure what else to do! In the House Churches you have a greater proportion of people with a pioneering spirit, otherwise we would not be here. So I am hoping that God is going to use that pioneering spirit in fresh initiatives in the Church, to take us into areas of social concern.

"I think that women could do a lot more than men. For example, many do not have full-time jobs, and also they often realise more quickly than men do what the concern is. Men often have to have it pointed out that there is a problem and they are often very shocked, whereas women, by virtue of the way they have been involved with the home and family, can pick up things a lot more quickly.

"Each woman needs to find out what God wants her to do. However, we don't all want to be rushing in, without the heartbeat of God, and starting something that we cannot continue, because it is not ideal letting people down. It is time to realise that we have the answer, and begin to affect some of these needy situations. It is going to cost us, in our homes. There will be some of us who have got to take some of these battered people into our homes and re-parent them. Obviously a married woman can't go into that without the backing and support of her husband and children, if they are old enough to understand what Mum is going to do.

"I feel if we do not get involved, we will just vegetate and become happy people, enjoying celebration, community and one another. Having done what God told us to do, becoming a community within a community, showing God's caring heart, with our sharing of things such as cars, washing machines and so on, we do not seem to have had the impact on the community that we would hope to have had. If our strength is our community and friendships, this could become our weakness, because we don't need other friends. As a result, we do not pursue our neighbours in the same sort of way as communities or churches that are not so tightly knit. There are very few who will have coffee or a meal with a neighbour. But these are some very simple ways to start. God needs to speak into the situation for us.

"However, if we are meant to be church planting, then we may need to lose a good third of our people to this as other new folk come in to be trained, nurtured and matured. As I move around the country, I do realise that we are very blessed in the calibre of life that is being lived in our community, even amongst our more problem-orientated folk. They might not necessarily all feel that to be true, but put them into a different setting with a different role and they will blossom, because their foundations are in, and only the building needs to go up.''

Jean Darnall shares that she is very keen to see people follow what God is doing today. Her past experience was very different. ''When I was growing up in the ministry, right until we came to Britain, ministry was preaching the gospel, praying for the sick, pastoring, but all this was with a spiritual emphasis. It was an 'other-worldly' Christianity. You came away from the world, touching not the unclean thing! We took away the effect of the salt and the light from the arts, politics and even from medicine.

''Then, during the charismatic renewal, I could hear the Holy Spirit calling people into these areas, to children in need, or against pornography, or bad housing, or what was happening through the media. This is how Festival of Light came about, which is now Care Trust. Today we see the Lord bringing redemptive grace into these fields and calling people into them, to bring in Christian taste, ethics, wisdom and morality. And I think women can be used in some of these areas more than men, because of their sympathy and tenderness and ability to stick with it when it is hard.

''Part of the renewal of the Church is the restoration of social concern within the ministry of the gospel. I don't know how we could have been so blind, because the New Testament is full of it. The teachings of Jesus include prison work, feeding the poor, clothing the naked, housing the homeless. He says that if we have done it unto one of those, we have done it unto Him. This is why God sends renewal and revival, because the Church develops blind spots. We cannot see the obvious. When the Holy Spirit comes, we begin to see it, even though it has always been there!''

Sylvia Mary Alison feels that it is very important for women to be involved in social action. She reflects, ''The heart of Christ is for suffering people and the helpless. He is grieved by these battered wives and children, and His heart of love, breathing through His people, wants to go out to cherish those people. One can feel guilty not doing anything about these problems, but you can't do everything. You have to do the bit the Lord shows you. If you are shutting your heart to the ones in pain, there is something very wrong. There is always a Lazarus at your gate.

"One thing that concerns me is that many feel that it is the Government's responsibility to do things. I believe this to be false. I think that the Lord said that if you are really a Christian you will go and do something about it yourself. If all the Church were really doing that, then the Government would not have a problem."

Everyone should be socially concerned, and do something when confronted with trouble, or when pain is being inflicted, rather than expecting someone else to take care of it. To take action further than that is more to do with gifting and ability and experience. We also need to be aware of demonic activity and the control exercised in such areas; what the Bible calls 'principalities and powers'. These forces need to be taken into account if God calls us into social work, and women are often gifted in discernment.

People have their own burdens in these areas too. Recognition of these burdens means that people are already motivated towards doing something. Pressure can come as time is taken from marriage and family relationships, but if God is calling us into social concern, husbands knowing this will be happy to take more responsibility at home to release us. There is always a cost involved.

Ruth Calver shares that she feels that the Church has dropped out of its responsibilities in the area of social involvement and action. "We have allowed people of many different persuasions to come in and take over the action. Men and women both need to be involved. I have become concerned in areas where my natural life has developed. So I am involved in the school and home situations. With four children, a busy husband and people living in my home, my horizon is limited and yet it is so vast.

"My first commitment is my children. I am on the PTA at our Church of England school, and I have just been elected the one parent-governor. For the last two years I have run the school prayer meeting. We have seen tremendous answers to prayer. Initially the head felt it would be divisive, but eventually allowed us to start praying for just three months. Now, she is constantly thanking us for prayers and the answers to prayer. We Christian parents tend to be the parents the head turns to in a crisis. If we have earned the right and shown our concern and commitment, we will have much more of a voice.

"Every woman should be concerned with some social action, even asking questions like, 'Why is our next-door neighbour not appearing out in the street, what is going on?' We should have eyes looking around the community in which we live. We need to get our children involved in caring for the neighbours too. We also need wisdom. If our caring concerns take too much energy and if I am too exhausted to give my children time, I must draw back. How much one should be involved depends on one's stage of development with one's children and the time available.

"These concerns certainly should be one of our top priorities, and not way down the list after meetings and committees and everything else. Jesus put a lot of emphasis on caring and He gave a high percentage of His ministry to feeding the hungry, caring for widows and orphans and children. It is great to see older people involved in this area as well. I know a woman recently widowed who loves taking books round to housebound people, which takes her out of herself."

Sue Barnett feels that it takes women to relate to women, and many of the social concerns need a woman's touch and understanding. "Jesus was involved with the body as well as the spirit, but there must be the balance. There has to be an investment of time in the lives of those we are trying to reach.

"My recent visits to a Scottish women's prison opened my eyes to the terrific opportunities there. It was one of the best hearings I've ever been given. 'Keep fit' proved to be a powerful short cut in relationships. I got to know them as people, and was able to share an all-round fitness that includes a relationship with God. I look forward to visiting them again.

"Our secular society is shouting that religion is redundant in our country. This is so right. Our country does not need religion, it cries out for reality. Reality is found in a relationship with the living God who created our country. We need to share the good news of Jesus and pray for our nation."

Marion White does not feel that the issue of social concern is a men and women issue. It is the whole Church that must be involved, and that means all of us. She continues, "It obviously depends on circumstances and where you live and what you are doing. We are in the country, so my area of involvement is in the school and PTA. There are always the one-to-one situations too, such as our neighbours and people we know around us. This is how God has us involved locally.

"In Open House we had little training when we started to take people in. We had a definite call in our lives and it was an on-the-job learning experience, based on our earlier experience of youth work. For us that was definitely a blend of being called and having had some experience.

"Within YFC, we are getting involved in the inner cities, and bringing youngsters out of the inner cities to help them by giving them a total experience at Cleobury, spiritual as well as mental and physical. I feel we need to be a voice and address certain issues. So we can also have a calling by God into some specific social action.

"I was speaking recently on this, saying that I'm tired of hearing people say they are going to get involved with drug addicts. They then charge in, find an unsuspecting drug addict and bring him home, and within weeks they cannot handle it. This is because they don't know a thing about drugs, or what the life of an addict is really like. They don't realise it is a life of lies, deception and dishonesty, and so they kick the person out. We then have another disillusioned and disheartened peron, as well as the Christian who also feels a failure. So although there are the very few clearly gifted and called people, most of us either need some experience or some knowledge of the thing before we jump in to be a 'do gooder'!"

Women should be involved no differently to the way men are. Some in the Church do not want to be known, for example, as women leaders. They would rather be known for their gift. The same should apply for any gift, including an ability to function in the area of social concern. The whole question needs to be looked at quite radically within the Church, without excluding the possibility that someone's employment might be changed. There are lots of schemes around where you can train, and with prayer backing in the Church, which is essential, and house-groups where you can talk through the things you are up against, there is a good foundation to proceed.

Bren Robson says, "People are looking for answers, and have become disillusioned with all kinds of other things. People are turning to the doctor and his surgery, the psychiatrist and his couch, the medium and her message, the guru and his religion, anywhere in fact where answers are being given. Young people will say things like, 'What is the point of obeying my parents, when they seem to do what they like themselves?' Or, 'What is the point of saving myself for marriage when I might be dead tomorrow in a nuclear holocaust?'

"I believe the Church has a rare opportunity to speak out, and to demonstrate the love of God in practical ways as well as speaking the truth. I feel women should be involved as much as they are called and are able to be, and on the same basis as men would be. Locally here we have become informed on some basic issues, but the next step has been to move into action teams. People have as a result become involved in the local community. The teams are not needed now as people are in place, involved in the community as individuals in various areas.

"Spearheading the formation of these action teams, within the church, the purpose was to build a bridge into the community, and each group had a separate function. As a result 20% of our church have moved into areas such as education, the anti-abortion issue, the media, work with the elderly, evangelism, street work and local politics. The whole operation was spearheaded by prayer. It is true to say that if we are functioning as we should be as Christians, we would not need these bridges.''

Grace Barnes is first concerned to ask the question, ''What would Christ have done, had He been physically present?'' She continues, ''I also have to be careful not to put a burden on people which they are not capable of fulfilling. We need to get down in prayer and fasting and ask God to raise people up who are the right people, for the right job. We must not jump too quickly, as a result of the situations around us. We must pray and find out God's heart. Men as much as women must be involved.

''We do have individual callings, and churches have callings too, but it is most important to be sent from the Church, with care and covering. Today I find more and more that God is sending people out in teams. The person in ministry on their own is now someone from the past. We are no longer meant to be left alone, out in the cold.

''God has already begun to move me out into the world. Having been to Africa, I am also in the process of making plans to take a team into Mexico. My burden is to take teams of women into these areas to stand with the people there and love them. Many are suffering as second-class citizens within their culture. I would like to minister to them and stand with them in prayer, believing that God will do something for them.

''I am now also very involved with an organisation which Norman founded called Links International. This was born out of a concern for the needs of people abroad. He went to Ghana, and saw at first hand, visiting a missionary's home, what life was like. They had one tin of meatballs between seven, with some rice. The children thought it was Christmas, because they were opening a tin of meatballs! Norman wrote down all the things they needed, and came home and shipped them out, including car parts. These missionaries need to be freed up to do the job they were called to do.

''So Links began, and we began to relate not directly to the non-Christians abroad, but rather to the Christians. They could then go to the non-Christians, after we had helped them with things that they could not do for themselves. We have helped by building a garage workshop for example, and sending out a printing press. We have been able to send out personnel who could train the local folk to use and service the printing press, which they could not do for themselves. So Links has helped me and many others get involved in the wider world.''

Anne Townsend feels that Christian women should be involved in training for work in social concerns as fully as possible. She concludes, ''One of our problems is that we are not trained in what to do, so we can offer a shoulder for people to cry on and a cup of tea, but we do not have the professional or technical expertise to know how to deal with some people with very sad problems in our churches, like the sexually abused child or a battered wife.

''Some of us could get this training. It is available in Christian and non-Christian set-ups. It is expensive to obtain, but maybe some churches could consider putting a large sum of money aside for one of their women to be trained, and then to come back and teach the rest of the church how to go about one of these jobs. We are generally seen by social workers as bungling and ineffective, and actually making things worse. I don't think that this is always a wrong judgement.

''Caring is something women are good at. It doesn't look or feel glamorous to be bathing the old, incontinent granny down the road regularly, but it is a significant way of practising what you preach. Most of us live in our little church ghettos, and we barely know people outside. We don't know our next-door neighbours as human beings. We may know them as people that we try and drag along to church meetings and try to get converted, but we have not actually loved Mr Smith next door because he is Jim Smith.

''Until we begin to do this, we are not going to begin to love and care for the world as Christ wants us to. We need to devote time and energy to building relationships, and building loving networks in our neighbourhoods. This may mean that some of the time we spend enjoying fellowship at church will have to be cut. But perhaps God is asking us to do this. It is in the joy and pain of living as people, and sharing our daily lives with others, that opportunities of sharing our faith are spontaneous and natural.

"Maybe some of us need to get out into secular jobs. If you have school-age children, you could do a part-time job in a supermarket or shop for three hours a day, getting to know non-Christians at their level, working alongside them, making friends with them, going to staff entertainments with them and having them back home. Then you will see where people are hurting and how Christ wants to minister to them. They are not going to come queuing up outside the church door.

"In my experience of speaking on social concerns, you are lucky if one person offers to do anything! It is almost impossible to get people to see beyond their own church and their own family. Sometimes in Care Trust, when pregnant girls have come to us (needing a family with whom to live until the baby is born), we have not been able to find a Christian family who could help in some areas of the 'Bible Belt' around London. Many families could not do this specialised work but most won't even *think* about it, and that is what worries me. It is sad that many people don't even pray, 'Lord make me care, if it is what you want me to do.'"

So what conclusions can we come to in this vast issue of social concerns? Obviously we have a long way to go. There seems to be a need for real corporate repentance. God commands justice for the oppressed. Jesus commanded us to 'go' into all the world. If we disobey His command, our attitude is suspect. We have been 'other-worldly' for too long. All mankind is made in God's image, despite sin. Men and women created in His image are crying out in need, in a hurting world.

Jesus wept over situations, people and places. We need to know something of His compassion. We will also gain compassion through our own experiences in life, so that we can comfort with the comfort we have been comforted with. If we go out into the world with this attitude, God will be able to use us.

Jesus' disciples were free to move about the regions and eventually into other countries. Many of the women remained local, especially those married with families to care for. Today, we are all missionary women able to touch our local area through relationships, schools, working with the elderly, hospital visitations, or whatever God lays on our hearts. We all have gifts within our character and personality, which will have outworkings in their own unique way.

We are called to be salt and light in the world. The need, however, does not justify the call. We cannot be everything to everyone. We need to hear from God individually and as churches concerning what He would have us do. Gaining experience and training as we move through the various stages of our lives equips us to answer the call when it comes.

Adam and Eve were together partakers of the divine nature. One sex alone can never communicate God adequately to the world. Only through men and women cooperating together will we eventually see God in all His fullness touching the world. One sex alone, as has so often been the case, gives a very strange picture of Christianity. So the 'togetherness' of Genesis needs to be restored. We need men and women who are dependent on God and on one another moving out secure together, to show God's love, care and concern for those in need in the world.

SECTION 4

IS IT POSSIBLE?

Nine

Women in Leadership

Today in the Church the question of women in leadership is one of the major issues. People are asking, "Can a woman in the Church lead, not only on the many committees of para-church organisations, but actually in the local church, alongside the men, even in terms of direction and government?" Perhaps we first need to ask, "What is leadership?" Many good books have certainly been written on the subject. Jesus, however, never defined leadership as male; His leadership was found in serving. He was the good shepherd who laid down His life for the sheep.

We are told elsewhere that a leader should be self-controlled, wise, able to impart vision, able to make decisions and carry them through, able to cope with failure, patient, self-sacrificing, able to delegate, able to make disciples and have an ordered life. None of these qualities appear to belong to one sex more than the other.

However, there are already two firmly held positions emerging. Some in the Church are against women leading because traditionally it has not been done before. They ask, "Why should women lead just because it is the end of the twentieth century?" Why indeed? But let us also ask, "Why are so many suddenly speaking in tongues, in the Church, at the end of the twentieth century?" Things are happening today, with the recovery of truth, that were unheard of a hundred years ago.

Pagan women have often been denigrated and few have moved into leadership positions. In Western culture we too expect male leaders. In the Church, in some circles, it is more acceptable for those leaders to be homosexual than female! Many feel that God is male, and therefore all leadership and authority in the Church is male — they give no place to the fact that God transcends sexuality, He is neither male nor female, He is both, and much more!

Others in the Church are seeing this whole issue as the next major area for reform. Women are seen out in the world, well able to lead. They are becoming educated and trained. In many churches in North America there is no problem concerning women in church leadership. A pastor's wife can automatically become a pastor in her own right after five years.

Elsewhere it has been quoted that some conservative politicians feel that Margaret Thatcher, whilst Prime Minister, was the best 'man' for the job available at the time in their ranks. So the question needs to be asked: is leadership really so male? When God calls women today, has He got it wrong? Or do men perhaps need to learn to cope with more gifted and anointed and able women in the Church, rather than remaining insecure and afraid of the consequences of changing attitudes?

The Bible gives us insight into women in leadership. In the Old Testament women seemed to have more freedom early on. It was later that oppression came, as the Israelites became tainted with other religions. Deborah consistently had God's word for people in her day. However, when she was called to make a response to Barak's weakness, she knew her limitations and gifts, and certainly did not take over the whole job herself (Judges 4:8). This is one picture of true leadership, and it is shown by a woman, who was part of a team.

We have Miriam too, often forgotten as a leader alongside Moses and Aaron (Micah 6:4). She was a praise and worship leader of repute. Esther, in her reign, led her nation through a devastating situation with both wisdom and perfect timing. She was given power and authority by the king (Esther 9:29). This is another picture of true leadership and authority. It cannot be grasped at, only given. It is something that others must recognise.

In the New Testament we find Jesus including women at every opportunity. It has been said that the only reason He may not have had female disciples was because, within His culture, it would have lost Him so much credibility that dialogue would have been impossible. We know, however, that Jesus did not do things simply to gain credibility, but nevertheless He had come to the lost sheep of the house of Israel and was reaching down into their culture at the end of an era, with a glorious chapter about to begin. We know how much He enjoyed sharing with Mary, who sat at His feet.

Paul too clearly wanted women to learn and be taught alongside men. This was contrary to the teachings of the rabbis, of whom he had been one. Rabbi Eleazer had said, ''Let the words of the law be burned, rather than given to a woman''! Yet Paul opened up the way for women to learn and grow in God, and what was the point of learning, if not to pass on their learning?

Paul's co-workers were often women who laboured with him in the gospel. These women, who had found the Lord, had grown enough spiritually to function alongside Paul in the Church. Had he not used women there might not have been a Roman Church! About thirteen men and ten women founded it. In Romans 16, the list shows his appreciation of many of these women. Junias, who was probably a woman, is named among the apostles. Priscilla is mentioned ahead of her husband Aquila more often than not, which means that she was a woman of note in her day. He sent Phoebe to Rome carrying the papers he had written, bidding the Church there to aid her in every way. It would be hard to believe that she did not speak to the Church on her arrival in Rome.

Elsewhere in the New Testament we are told that Timothy was taught in the faith by his mother and grandmother. In Lydia's house the Church started with women. So, in the New Testament, we have many liberated ladies. In fact, all through history, women have pushed back the boundaries imposed upon them and taught the gospel to people near and far.

Today, we have Christian women beginning to function at all levels of leadership. It is interesting to hear how the Holy Spirit is leading some of them and what they think and feel about this whole issue at this moment in time. What they are learning can be passed on, so that we can be both encouraged and perhaps learn from their difficulties. We do not all have to make the same mistakes repeatedly; we can learn from one another's lives.

Jill Dann, being the chair of the Church of England Evangelical Council, feels that leadership needs to be shared and mixed with different gifts, and exercised where possible by people of different sexes, different ages and different colours. She explains, ''People must not be threatened by women in leadership. The only worries I would have would be those I would have about men in leadership. We don't want status-seekers. We desperately need people like Jesus, who said that He was there as one who serves, and not the kind of people who just stand up in front and say, 'Follow me!'

''In the early years of my marriage, as we did not worship in an evangelical church, we had to work out our faith for ourselves. We had to get down to the Scripture as a whole, not just odd texts. We were in a place where women were not expected to do anything. They were pleased that I could add up and so made me Treasurer! So I was able to do something that was traditionally a male job. There is a tendency to concentrate on what women may not do, rather than on what they can do. Praying and prophesying does not fit in with being quiet and doing nothing. I came from a background of a Brethren girls' Bible class, and unspoken rules at university where as a woman you did not do certain things, as opposed to being encouraged to do anything positive.

''Not wanting to write off the negative texts, I would rather start the other way round. Romans is so full that you don't often reach chapter 16, but when you get there you see how Paul, who had not even been to Rome, sent greetings and over a third of these fellow workers in the gospel were women. So I cannot be anti-Paul, because he is so positive. He came from a rabbinical background, where women were nothing, yet he was so changed by Christ that he was accepting women as fellow workers. His first convert was a

woman — Lydia, whose home he visited — and he sent
Apollos to learn from Priscilla. He was not anti-women.

"Phoebe is mentioned as a deaconess in most translations,
but in fact it is the neuter word 'deacon', not a female word
at all. In 1 Timothy 3:11, where it talks about 'the wives of
deacons', there is no possessive pronoun in any manuscript
at all, and so it probably refers to women deacons. It is not
certain, but to have women deacons at this stage was pretty
revolutionary! If Paul had thought women were incapable
of teaching, and easily deceived, he would not have praised
these women. It is not possible in so short a space as this
to look at the different texts.

"I think in England we have a lot of men who are insecure.
They have to keep a stiff upper lip, and are not allowed to
be emotional. This affects them in their relationships with
women. They are often threatened by us, without knowing
it. It is much easier for them if they can keep their picture
of what a woman is as a stereotype, either at the kitchen sink,
or in bed, certainly 'at home'. Too often they are uneasy when
they find women with gifts that they don't know how to cope
with. This is where mixed education is good, particularly at
sixth-form level. It opens things up for both sexes.

"Men tend to feel that the women out pioneering on the
mission field are odd women. I have had something of this
thrown at me. People have said that I am more like Deborah
in the Old Testament. To this I say that I am no different to
many women — I have just had more opportunities, and
many women, given those same opportunities, would do the
same as I have done. There is no distinctiveness in the
ministry a woman might have, as compared to a man, but
probably the way that she exercises it will be different from
the way a man would do it."

Christine Noble, who is a well-known conference speaker
and ministers internationally, feels the same about women
in leadership as she does about men. She shares what she
means. "Women should be there just the same as men,
because God has put gifts of leadership within them, and that
is the only reason for being in leadership. There are many
areas and levels of leadership. A definition of leadership is

having others following and falling in behind you, whether
it be a cell group, a church, a city or a nation. If people see
leadership qualities, and that the person is in touch with God,
they believe they can trust the way the person is moving.
If you are not gifted in leadership, you will quite likely have
a nervous breakdown in that role! Leading in the Church can
be a painful experience.

"For me, the 'difficult' Scriptures in 1 Timothy 2:11-14 and
1 Corinthians 14:34-35 have been taken out of context. In
those situations the women were ignorant and illiterate. Their
questions were so basic and ridiculous, answering them in
public would have wasted time. It was not that they must
not question what was said, but that they should do it at
home. In their culture it was the norm for every woman to
be married, and they had an educated man they could refer
to. Jewish boys really were taught the Scriptures, so a woman
knew that her husband had understanding. Actually Paul
goes right against his culture, and as a rabbi encourages
women to learn, but to be quiet for that learning period of
time. However, you cannot pray and prophesy in church with
your mouth shut! So, they were not to be silent for ever —
they would soon be moving in God's gifts."

Grace Barnes, who is also well known for organising
women's conferences and her involvement with churches in
other countries through Links International, feels that she has
no problem in this area. She says, "I feel men and women
in leadership need to work in a team. It is good when the
team is mixed on occasions. At other times, women can work
together as a team, for example, at our women's retreats.
Once we move as individuals, independently of one another,
that can really spell trouble.

"Priscilla and Aquila were used together as equals in
ministry and were both teachers. This would seem to
contradict Paul's words elsewhere about women being silent
and not teaching. So we must understand his context, as he
obviously allowed Priscilla to teach. Concerning the word
'silence', we find there are two kinds of silence in Scripture.
The Greek word which is used twice is *hesuchia*, meaning
'stillness and quietness', 'to be peaceful', 'keeping one's

seat', 'being undisturbing in life and language'. This is not the same silence as used in Acts 21:40 or Revelation 8:1. That silence was *sige*, which means 'to hiss' or 'to hush'.

"We must get the right kind of silence for our understanding of this passage. If we took the word 'silence' literally today, we would not sing, pray in meetings, or even teach in Sunday School. So there must be a further meaning or, as was recently said to me, we would take our shoes off so that we would not make a noise on the floor! The word has to have a different meaning, and be applicable for those in authority too, who need to have a stillness of spirit and be undisturbed by strife and disorder."

Learning in silence with submissiveness is an incredibly hard thing for some women to do, particularly if there is no husband at home to speak to. Also, if you are not taught to read and write, as missionaries abroad have found, then the mouth, ears and eyes are the primary means of learning. Linked together with the fact that New Testament women were now on an equal footing with men, in a male-dominated society, these factors produced an overall problem.

"There was an exuberance at finding in Jesus all that He meant for womanhood. So there were many questions. Was a woman going to start behaving like a man? Because she did not know how to behave, should she interrupt and ask questions as some men did? Paul spoke into this situation to stop disorder; a situation very different to those in our twentieth-century Church history, where women have been silenced in some fellowships and denominations.

Jean Darnall, who has a well-known international ministry, has been preaching and teaching now for over fifty years. From her experience she says, "Reading all those verses in 1 Timothy 2 to the end, verse 15 seems to sound as though through bearing children women will be saved! But we know that the rest of Scripture does not agree with that and if you took it out of context and preached it, we would say that it was false doctrine. Taking just verses 11 and 12 and making a whole teaching out of that does not consider the context at all. For instance, in 1 Corinthians 11:5, Paul talks about women prophesying with their heads covered, in other words as long as they are in the proper attitude of submission.

"So we must see that the 1 Timothy 2 Scriptures are not a rule. Putting this in the light, with all the women that Paul allowed to minister, and those he appointed, shows a broader picture. For example, in Cloe's house it is apparent that she is in charge. As for those two other women that were apparently leaders of some sort, Paul wanted to see them getting on together, although they had difficulty in their relationship. So he was acknowledging women.

"I feel also that the word 'silence' in verse 11 does not mean complete silence. Within the synagogue context, where Paul did a lot of his teaching, the women were still divided from the men. Elmer and I once went to a synagogue where you could hear the women whispering upstairs. Downstairs, as the men were reading from the scrolls, men in the congregation would speak up and ask questions. This was while the reading was going on, and the reading would stop and be explained and then a little more would be read. So it is an altogether different kind of church order, where discussion is acceptable, and Paul was probably saying that these women did not yet know enough to make a really good discussion. They needed to listen and learn and not to take authority over men.

"It seems to me that it is a matter of attitudes all the way. Paul may have had to deal with a very pushy woman, who was trying to dominate a weak male leader! I have seen that happen! Women also tend to respond more quickly to the moving of the Spirit, and I think that, as a result, Paul may have had some nervousness here. He was speaking into Timothy's church situation particularly. Timothy seems to have been quite a shy person. Paul talks to him and says, 'Don't let anyone despise your youth.' He must have been an ulcer type, with some sort of stomach trouble. So I think Paul was really defending Timothy, telling him to be careful, and not let strong women walk all over him. They can kill you off before you have a chance to get going!

"I know a pastor who went into a church with a very small congregation. God began to bless it and bring in new people. He noticed that in the operation of the gifts, the women were much more forward, and so he asked the women in the church, whenever there was a message in tongues, that they wait longer than they ordinarily would, to give the men a chance to give the interpretation. He also asked them, if they felt a prophecy, to pray that the Lord would use a man.

"He felt that if they did not do this, all the vocal gifts would be operating through women and it would not be a healthy balance, and he wanted the men to develop too. The women knew that he respected them and therefore they could receive this. As a consequence that church has produced some very strong men with wonderful ministries. The women also have matured, and there is not the competitive feeling on the women's part or laziness on the men's part of letting the women do it. Today, that fellowship numbers several thousand."

General Eva Burrows, who heads the Salvation Army, confirms that her style of leadership is a feminine style. "I call it 'consensus in the Spirit', because I like to work in a group. Although I have great authority in the Salvation Army, I very much appreciate other people's ideas. I do not have a sense of lack of worth about my ideas, but I do know that mine are not the only ones.

"We now talk about consultative leadership in the Salvation Army. I may lead from up front, but I do not lead from a position too far ahead. I like my people to be with me. At the end of any discussion, I am not afraid to make the decision. I have learned much from the times when I have failed. I know that the greatest learning experiences in life can result from failures and finding meaning in them.

"Yes, I am well educated and think deeply about life. I don't take a pride in my education, as I see it only as a means to develop the mind that I have. I give far more credence to what I call 'sanctified common sense'. In other words, knowledge is only of value if it is useable. I have several other gifts that have also enabled me to lead. One is in the area of communication. Another is as a missionary. I also have the capacity to identify with people, as I feel for them in their difficulties. I have had the gift of leadership evident in my life since my childhood.

"We as Christians have an advantage over business people in the world. They are often fighting to get their own ideas accepted. Here in this forum, we are seeking what God wants for our growth and development. I try to show everyone in the group that I lead that they have their own self-worth, and I esteem other personalities and views and enjoy commending colleagues for their good ideas.

"Masculine leadership can be rather competitive. I think men are more interested in organisation and management and even their career structure. Women are different and although I would not call myself emotional, I think that emotions are very important. It is what you feel that usually mobilises you to action. Therefore, I make no apologies for feelings of the heart, as well as feelings of the mind. I feel a woman's style in management is often quite disarming, as opposed to confronting. We like to start with a warm relationship that we can build on. Most women usually try to break down the barriers first, before moving on."

So it is apparent that there are other ways to persuade than simply by being macho or domineering. There are other ways to make decisions than simply imposing hierarchical structures. There are other ways of coming to the truth than simply pronouncing. Women should resist appeasement, whether by traditional feminine ways or by silence. We must believe in our own convictions and have the courage to speak in love to, or in front of, those more senior than ourselves.

Bren Robson's experiences lead her to feel that a negative reaction from a man towards a woman in leadership is often not reasoned at all, but illogical. She feels, "Honest questions about women in leadership or any other issue can be answered and reasoned through together. But so much of our difficulty in this comes from our own problem, weakness or prejudice.

"Because we have denied so much for so long in our particular society, we are sometimes unable to be objective. It is as though we look through glasses (as when we look through completely red spectacles, and we see the colour green as black) of repression, prejudice, history and culture.

We are then not able to be reasoned and open. The enemy has moved in with spirits of enmity and division. He is determined to keep men and women apart, when they actually function best together. It is interesting to note that in every other religion, women are debased to the point of having no rights at all in some cases.

"Men and women still have a responsibility in all this because we have allowed it to happen. In my view, there will always be a struggle for women to lead, because we live in a fallen world, and that struggle will go on until Jesus wraps up this present age. Our negative reaction to women in leadership, as in any other issue, is partly to do with the curse, as a result of sin entering the Garden of Eden. Although we can appropriate freedom from the curse for ourselves, we shall always have a struggle, in the world in which we live, to lead and to be free as women, and as men and women working together.

"In 1 Timothy 2, women were becoming aware of areas that had hitherto been denied them. It is likely that in their enthusiasm they were grasping at authority, not yet having learned right attitudes. I would say the same to new Christians today. They should not be the ones in church eldership or the leadership team. New Christians need to be disciplined and apprenticed, learning in quietness with all submission, without making a disturbance in the meetings and shouting out.

"We need to define what we mean by 'women in leadership'. It seems to mean different things to different people. Leadership is holding current responsibility in the kingdom of God, whether it is in the local church or further afield. (I would want to pay tribute to those men and women who have sought to pioneer, so that women are now sometimes free to minister and lead. There are still very few in places of influence, especially when it comes to policy shaping or being in the public arena.)

"Personally I am encouraged by the signs of things beginning to happen, and delighted that there are men of influence in the House Church willing and committed to the promotion of women as well as men. Men are going to need to pioneer, to give women place in this area of leadership.

In history I have not found anywhere where a man has voluntarily given up his position, and certainly if he has, it would have been a struggle. Men in positions of authority are needed to give an 'overemphasis' to giving women place, because authority cannot be taken, only given. If this does not happen then women will never get the experience that they need. So I would want to encourage some men to take risks. Some of us women will flunk it, but then some men flunk it too.

"Meanwhile women need to prepare women to take their proper place, overcome fears and inferiority, preparing to be able and faithful in areas of ministry and leadership — just as, in the New Testament, once women had learned and been apprenticed, they were given place. I believe it is possible to give women the same place today. I believe men and women work best together, because together they make up the image of God. I enjoy being a person in leadership and feel comfortable in a man's world, so long as I can be a woman in it! I think it is important that as women we do not try to be men.

"We do need to be practical. I remember going to a leaders' prayer meeting, for a very big celebration evening. One of the male leaders asked us to lead out in prayer. But because there was so much noise, it would have been totally impossible for a woman to lead in prayer, because she does not have the volume! We must address these kind of issues, and perhaps adjust where possible.

"Reaction experienced against such issues as this tends to polarise men and women. We need to guard against this. At the same time, because we are pioneering there will be reaction, which we need to expect and accept. This has happened all through history, when truth has been recovered. One of the reactions in women that I am concerned about is in those women who have struggled for years in a place of unnecessary subservience, only to discover that in fact they can now have a freedom they never thought possible. Many of them find this difficult.

"It is vitally important that women who want to take responsibility are not pushed away from the Church. We have in the past pushed them into the mission field and now some are looking for other avenues outside the Church. My plea is this: let's allow women place in the Church, where there is safety and boundaries, with men and women who can support them, so that we do not become individualistic, isolated and bitter.''

Pat Cook is the executive director of the Central Asian Mission. She feels strongly that, particularly amongst many charismatic fellowships, there are women with real gifts, and the men do not know how to recognise these gifts, often because they do not know how to handle the issue of women in leadership. She continues, ''In part this problem arises because women can be more emotional than men. But the leadership gift is no more exceptional than any other gift. It is just one of the gifts in the Church. Outside the whole concept of the ordination of women, which is another subject altogether, some women need to be developing their leadership gifts, until the church recognises their gift and puts them into the place of leadership. Local church recognition is essential.

''I do not feel it is the norm for women to be in leadership all the time. God has not planned for women always to lead men! But as God moves in many different ways, He has obviously given some women the gift of leadership both inside and outside the Church. They must be encouraged to function under covering. The greatest hindrance, however, is stroppy, bossy women leaders! So some women who have the gift of leadership need teaching and training in how to handle it.

''When some people say, for instance, that you find a woman running the Church because there is no man, I rather see, in God's perfect plan, that He sometimes gives the gift of leadership to a woman, which cannot be denied. Some women have outstanding leadership ability with Spirit-filled ministry, but I do not feel it is the norm for women to be ordained ministers of the Church. I have seen a woman move out in leadership in a meeting context, when it has been her area of ministry, and humbly take the initiative when no one else knew what to do in a given situation. She went to the microphone in order that people could be helped, and no one could deny that they saw God in that woman, as she took up leadership during that time.

"I find it quite difficult to be picked out as a woman leader. I have now come to the conclusion that I am not the leader of CAM because there is not a man to do it, but rather because God wants me there and has given me the gift and ability to do it. I am often asked why I am leading in the mission work that I am involved in. My answer is always that God has called me to do it. If people do not feel it is biblical, I say to them that I feel their conclusion is wrong. Sometimes I say to such people, how about asking God about it? The norm in God's plan is that men are generally leaders, but there are the exceptions to the rule, and God has given some women gifts of leadership. I feel I am one such woman.

"When I first moved out in leadership, I thought I had to make myself known, but I found out that this is not true. It is rather the servant role I have had to take. In the struggles, my own heart has been touched and challenged into becoming a servant heart. I do appreciate the struggle that men are having with this issue, as they have their own struggles with domineering women around them who want to control things. This does not stop me believing in women in leadership, confirmed by the local church."

Authority comes from respect. The worst caricature is the image of a domineering woman, but that is because a domineering man is sometimes excused because somehow he is strong, and strength is masculine. This produces a pressure in women in leadership to operate like men. We have not yet reached the day when women will not continually have to prove themselves *better* than men in order to be acceptable in leadership roles, when they don't have to be superwomen but can simply be women. However, verbalising the problem is a precursor to change. In the Church we always talk about what we are not yet into, but what we shall soon be moving into!

Sylvia Mary Alison is well known for her work in Prison Fellowship and now chairs the board of that organisation. She has never desired to be a leader and does not describe herself as one! She explains, "I have always been surprised at being a leader — not characterwise, because of being a head girl at school, which in the early days I tried to lose because of its bossy image. Rather I'm surprised that I am leading in any public way. Once I did a test where the aim was to find out what gifts people had. In that test I came out as a leader. The gift of leadership is, for me, just to bring on other people, and to spot the gifts in others. I am also able to spot the next leader, and stay there until it is time for her to become leader, and then hand it on.

"My leadership, which is outside the Church, has not happened because the Church has not actually enabled me to be in leadership in the church unit as such. I believe the Church is there to encourage the laity to work in the world. Why should anybody go to church, unless somebody meets them and shares the relevance of Christ? So I go to church to share in communion and worship, but not to sit about there. My calling is not to pastor or build the Church, rather it has been in private houses and in prisons. But I need to go back frequently to the refreshment of meeting with the Body of Christ.

"I asked God, at the time I was made chairman of Prison Fellowship, why He had put me in that position. A picture came, first of a hothouse plant with one bloom on top and the rest of the plant foliage. This is one sort of leadership, where you look at the leader. Then the picture developed. The way to make this shrub blossom is to snip off that bloom so that the strength goes into the rest of the plant. Then there are blossoms all over!

"I was that sort of leadership. I knew nothing about prisons, the system, fund raising or anything. So I have always had to turn to other people and say, 'You are the person who is good at this, can you do it?' I certainly bring people in, because I don't mind admitting I don't know things. This also frees everyone else up into giving their contribution, whether it be finance or our work in the regions. We are a team. If I really do not know what to do, we have a very good consultant whom I consult to find out the best way forward. I know that I am totally dispensable and if I am not there, it will not make any difference to Prison

Fellowship.

The Lord has used me to share visions and ideas. For ages I wanted a ministry and a function in the Body of Christ, when I was a housewife with small children. I longed to speak, but about what? The verse that really struck home to me was the one about 'speaking in exhortation'. Encouragement is one translation, or you exhort other people to see something. It is what the Americans would call inspirational!

"So now what I do when I share is say, 'Look, it is an exciting thing that God is wanting to do. It is like this.' Then people respond, 'Oh, I can do that, or I can do this.' Starting Prison Fellowship was like this. I went around sharing with groups that I felt the Lord wanted me to go to. Then afterwards I would find all sorts of things would begin to happen. The Lord was doing it; all I was doing was sharing the picture."

Talking about the verse in 1 Timothy 2, **Sylvia Mary** was very honest. "For years I felt in bondage to it. I mean I felt I must keep quiet, if there was a group of men in our sitting room praying. I would not pray in front of them. Then someone explained it to me, that the women in the New Testament were not to be allowed to shout out, 'I haven't understood what you mean, would you explain it again!' I do not have a gift of teaching; I only share with men if they ask me to, so I know they are going to listen or they would not have bothered to ask.

"I must confess that before I was involved with the Nationwide Initiative on Evangelism in the late 70s, I did have a hankering to be ordained. The reason was that I wanted a ministry that was publicly accepted amongst colleagues, so that people would take me seriously, whereas who takes a housewife seriously? But then the need for ordination ceased; as I began to work on the NIE, I realised that I would be much more useful without a label, much more able to be fluid and available.

"I wonder if half of the women who want to be priests are single women who have not got a husband's covering or life to belong to, and feel they have got to be accepted in the male community, which may be the wrong reason. Or perhaps they are moving out of frustration. I have certainly been frustrated, which has been resolved by my having a role in leadership, having something to contribute and having male colleagues. They don't feel I'm a threat, and I have ceased to desire to be ordained. I feel the Lord has set me apart for ministry and I feel secure in myself. People who feel insecure need a stamp.''

Anita Traynar is now involved with Christians In Education, having been administrator for Team Spirit. She shares that she has always felt that when Paul wrote to Timothy, he was basically getting at an attitude. ''It was written because of the cultural revolution that was happening, because of Jesus' teaching being outworked. I do feel that if the world is going to see a true picture of God, then you have got to have both male and female in leadership, because in the Godhead the whole aspect of these two personalities is wrapped up.

''So for me, if the Church has a totally male-dominated leadership, it is really missing the heart of Paul, and more importantly the heart of God. Those who believe in total male leadership are saying that the male personality is above deception and all those weaknesses Paul is denoting. But we know those weaknesses can occur as much in a male as in a female person. For me any team — and 'team' is the operative word more and more in the Church, rather than the one-man ministry — any team would be incomplete without women. I would still feel uncomfortable, for my own subjective reasons, if the leader of that team was a woman, and would find it difficult. But I feel there is a need for women on the team.

''I have sat under women teaching and preaching with the authority of God, where you would not question their spirits, because there is no way that they are lording it over the men or anybody. They know they are called of God, standing competent in that ability, and it comes over in just sharing the Word of God, and allowing the Holy Spirit to do what He will with it. On the other hand, you can sit in a congregation where you have a man who is a true, out-and-out authoritarian and does exactly what Paul was worried about, but because he has trousers on, it seems to be more acceptable! So it is all a question of attitude.

"Apart from anything else, women view things in a different manner. For example, I was recently involved in organising a conference for the first time, but there were some major errors in the preparation, because the leadership had not involved any women. It was simple things like the provision of meals for speakers, and toilet facilities with feeding mothers in mind — things which help with the running of an event but which, with the best will in the world, men do not think of! So our viewpoint can be helpful to the men.

"However it is not just always on a practical level, but spiritually as well that we have a role to play. We need to be listened to, because often we women can see more where a thing is going to than the men who are caught up in the nitty-gritty. We can share our concerns there and then. This is not just a male and female issue. It is also about the gifts and talents and abilities of the team, which need to be in balance."

Submission should permeate all our leadership. Both men and women should be like Christ, with servant hearts. The servant heart comes through to us as we read of the New Testament women such as the woman who broke the alabaster box over Jesus' head. Mary sat at His feet as a disciple and He probably listened to what she said. Jesus honoured this attitude among the women and even allowed a woman to be the first person to witness His resurrection, the most amazing event of all history! This is all the more remarkable because no woman could ever be a witness in court in those days.

Rosemary Andrews feels there are countless ministries open to us women that we should pursue, but our femaleness would fit us for some jobs better than others. She explains, "Many women are good pastors and teachers and if their husbands recognise this, they can support them and give recognition. If a woman decides to lead beside her husband, then they can be a team together. It may mean breaking down prejudice, but it is worth keeping going, under the Lord's guidance, as you may pioneer something new. I have found in my experience, that if husband and wife are a team ministry, then sometimes the husband will take the lead and sometimes the wife.

"We have to submit to one another, and both must hear from the Lord. I have had much encouragement from men, as well as a few hard knocks from some who felt threatened, but I am determined to press on by God's grace into what He wants me to do. Husbands and wives need to work together much more — there are too many unhappy situations where the wife longs to be beside her husband and yet protocol does not allow it. Too many Christian leaders' marriages break up because the husband has too much responsibility and limelight, while the wife is in the shadows. I honestly can't think that this is part of God's plan. Priscilla and Aquila worked and ministered together.

"The normal practice in New Testament times had been for women to leave it to the men to learn. It was a new day for these women who, until then, had not been considered worth teaching! Now women were freed up to learn and so Paul had to instruct them on how to respond. The emphasis that is always put forward on not letting a woman teach is 1 Timothy 2:14, which tells us that it was not Adam who was deceived, but the woman. This puts women in condemnation and confusion straight away. According to Genesis 3, the result of sin was to blame the other party! A woman should be thoroughly taught in the basic doctrines of the Word. She should then know how to respond to those teaching false doctrines, and not be led astray as Eve had been.

"Personally I have experienced conflicts in my own mind during my Christian walk and have often tried to resolve them by conforming to the cultural status quo, which can sometimes be necessary. However, instead of playing roles we should honestly and with true humility aim to express God's life in us to the fullest potential, never losing our zeal for Him."

Pat Tomlinson, who is the administrator for Team Work,

says that she too feels the same about women as she does about men who are in leadership. She continues, "I think there will be good and bad, and it has all got to be handled properly. Women have to go the same way men have come through in the past into leadership. They have to move and function as much as they can and are given place to do so. They should not expect men to do everything and give them all the openings. It is a dual thing, as women are given place; if they don't move ahead, they won't be given more place, with the chance to develop as men have done.

"I think the subject of authority has been built up tremendously by men. I would not view authority in the same light as it possibly has been viewed in the past. I think that real authority is when someone recognises something in you, and listens to what you have got to say, and then does something as a result of that. It is not something you go around wielding. I think that a God-given authority is something you earn, whether through counselling or the way you are with people.

"I believe there is special authority for particular leaders, but I don't think that would rule out other people having authority in different areas. It is a little difficult for me to see how this will work out in a woman in ultimate leadership, because we have not seen it yet. I do not think a woman would want a one-woman ministry. We are moving more and more towards teams. Women just want to be heard and have things they say considered, just like any man would. It may be that women moving into leadership will just change the whole ethos of male dominance and bring it into a more balanced type of leadership. Dave believes in woman elders, but I am not sure what that will look like.

"I have always thought deep down that I would like to be an elder, but what I am actually saying is that I would like to be there where the decisions are made, to put my thoughts and ideas across and have a part in what decision comes out. Not that I want my decision to go forward or anything pushy like that. I just feel I have something to give into that level. The few women who are in eldership now are working alongside the men in eldership, and this is how it needs to develop in the future.

"There is often a slight overemphasis on a new thing before it is brought into balance. I don't think you can skip this hurdle with something new, although it would be good if you could! One Anglican friend of ours had different elders responsible for different areas of church life, which is one way of approaching it. He has women amongst the men at this level. Also, eldership is not for life. There are often reasons why a man might want to drop out of eldership after a period. Perhaps his job has become more demanding, and he needs to pursue that. Our Anglican friend renews eldership regularly, which I think is healthy. I think if we let someone be an elder for ever, it allows people to get a bit sloppy.

"In the Bible I have my heroes! Esther is one. She moved into a position of leadership where she could put the word in at the right time, and that did the trick. I would really model myself upon people like her. She helps me, because we seem today to want to be having an effect on things all day, every day. To bring that one thing out in Esther's life is so crucial — being in the right place at the right time, saying the right thing, and for me it takes the heat out of having to produce something all the time. You just need to be where you are, at the right time, and bring what you have got and what you feel.

"I love the passage in Proverbs too, about the virtuous woman who obviously, in buying a field, had a job. She was a very liberated woman who achieved a lot, without necessarily doing it all herself. This speaks of being an effective leader in a household too. Her husband was elevated to his position because of all that she was doing. He was known as her husband, not she as his wife. What you are elevates your husband."

Some understand the verse in 1 Timothy 2 in the context of the husband-and-wife relationship. In that scripture in the Greek, the same word is used for a husband or a man, or a wife or a woman. So the words can mean 'women don't usurp' as well as 'wives don't usurp'. A wife should not usurp her husband's authority, because elsewhere she is told to submit to him. A woman exercising the wrong sort of authority is crushing and unhelpful. Equally, a man doing the same thing has a similar effect. If we have authority in a recognised area, it will be manifested to good effect.

"There are times when it is necessary for women to teach, because they are teaching on subjects that men know little about. For instance, if you are going to have a session on abortion or contraception or very feminine issues, you require teaching to be done by women. But there are also times when it is necessary for a woman to teach because she has a teaching gift. If this is recognised and she is invited to teach, she is usurping no one's authority!

Ruth Calver is involved in leadership amongst the women in the Ichthus Fellowship in South-East London. She shares concerning some of her difficulties, "When I came into our present fellowship, Clive was not going to be in any leadership. One day, I said to the leader's wife that I would find it very hard not being a leader's wife. She replied to me that it didn't matter whose wife you were. She said, 'You are you, and if you show the qualities you will be in leadership!'

"People often say of me, 'Oh, she is Clive Calver's wife, therefore she should be able to do this and that!' So what! It may not be what the Lord has told me to do, or gifted me in. Does the vicar's wife have to run the Mother's Union? Of course not. If the man is in leadership it does not necessarily mean that the woman is too. So many women today are taking on roles that God has not ordained for them, just as a result of being married to some Christian leader.

"For myself, I must be supporting Clive's ministry first as opposed to my own ministry at this time. If I am too busy to be a wife to him and keep the home together, then I must just cut down. I have had to be very secure in knowing that, especially when people find it hard that I am not at lots of meetings. I am giving out in all sorts of other places, and often need to be at home when the meetings are on. The meeting situation can be totally dominating, and as churches grow the meetings grow and escalate!

"As much as I am very pro the family, even that can do damage to one's own personality and self-esteem. You go through the nappies, the breast-feeding, and you are with children all day. If your husband is away a lot, you may not talk to an adult at all, for long periods. You can come out of this feeling you have not offered anything other than changing nappies for years. At this stage you have to rebuild. You may not have had a lot of time to study the Bible, because you have been taken up with so much else demanding your attention. So you have to learn again, and be encouraged to do it.

"Prior to having my children I could easily stand up and speak at a meeting, quite confidently. I've had to relearn that and get down to basic preparation. Going to Spring Harvest with the children, and finding I had to go to prayer meetings and counsel people, I could no longer hide behind the children!

"I am not for women just getting on the feminist kick and aggressively taking over leadership. Neither am I pro one-man or one-woman ministries. Whatever the situation in leadership, we need to be in teams, where we are knocking the rough edges off one another, and correcting each other. Often in churches where women are suppressed it is at home that the men are suppressed! The women are the battle rousers, while the men remain weak and do not take the lead in the family. If women are gifted and have something to offer and the Church is not allowing them to do it, I think that, rather than getting frustrated, it is better to leave and move on to where God leads, although I would not normally encourage people to give up so easily.

"Each couple has to find their calling in God. I can think of a couple in our fellowship, where initially the husband was house-group leader, and his wife was beside him. As the group developed, she was so obviously more gifted in that way than he was. Now she is very much involved in the leadership here in the fellowship and he is on the administrative side, doing a tremendous job, but not in leadership out front.

"A lot of people are craving leadership, whereas in fact in Scripture, leaders were often very reluctant people, for example: Moses, Gideon, Solomon, Joshua and also Jeremiah. God gave them all a job to do, and they made all sorts of excuses! God had to thrust them into leadership. That is not always the case, but many people have battles and have to be thrust out.''

Valerie Griffiths, after many years on the mission field, has returned to England with her husband and now lectures at London Bible College. She shares, from her own understanding, what she feels about the issue of women in leadership in the Church today. ''Our capacity for turning truth upside down is nowhere more evident than in the matter of leadership. Church history is a sad record of human values and aspirations dominating Christian communities.

''The history of Israel was a long period of turning from the basic tribal society where all people were equal before God, in covenant relationship with Him. Within a couple of centuries the society divided into social strata, ruler and ruled, rich and poor, and one group used their power for their own benefit and exploited the other group. Greed and desire for power always drive people in this direction, and Jesus rejected outright the lordship of Gentile kings over their subjects.

''If we were more aware of the psychological implications of power and authority, we would be much slower to claim it. The word authority is so abused. Jesus instead said the truly great are ready to let go of power and position and become like the youngest, and the leaders must become servants. As Luke 22:27b says, 'I am among you as one who serves.' This is the basic meaning of 'minister', yet we have given that word connotations of authority. In human hands hierarchy, authority and power are potentially destructive. Few human beings have the wisdom to handle them. Jesus said, 'Do not lord it over one another as the Gentiles do.' That kind of exaggerated authority is pagan.

''Jesus associated leadership with servanthood, and greatness with the humility of small children (Matthew 18:4). Philip King, in his book *Leadership Explosion*, points out that when we are told to obey God and civil leaders, the strong Greek verb *peitharcheo* is used. But when it comes to obeying church leaders, a weaker verb *peitho* is used, with the sense of being persuaded by reason, convincing and exhorting being implied. Again church members are to be subject to leaders, ranking themselves under and respecting them.

"The Christian family does not order itself on blind obedience and absolute authority. The leaders are urged to see that things are done decently and in order. They are to act decisively against serious heresy and immorality (2 John 9-11). But apart from that, the words are gentler, exhorting as a father, encouraging (1 Timothy 5:1), coming alongside with a message (1 Timothy 4:11) and gently instructing (2 Timothy 2:24-25). Tiller and Birchall, in their book *The Gospel Community*, refer to the fact that Christ gave authority to minister to the whole church with particular gifts bestowed on each individual, including leadership gifts.

"It is most unlikely that the 'leading women' of society in Antioch of Pisidia, Thessalonica and Beroea had to submit to the newest converted male slave when they believed. The Christian faith was revolutionary enough without overturning the structures of contemporary society. Priscilla was a leader with her husband. Phoebe was an administrator, a patroness and a woman of status. A surprising number of women are mentioned as colleagues and fellow workers in Romans 16. The churches met in the homes of Nympha and Priscilla.

"Leadership is a very general word. There are many different styles and forms. Many women have found themselves leaders when they never expected it, but in using the gifts the Holy Spirit gave them, and going where the Lord led, they have ended up leading others. Some leaders are given an official position or status by others, to do a particular work. Some are looked up to for their skill, knowledge and experience. Some have the gift for discerning the times and the way ahead, and can point others in that direction, who then 'give them authority' that they never sought.

"At creation both male and female were called to be stewards of God's world, to rule over it. Women have been created with their own special gifts, and for centuries these have been devalued as 'weaknesses' and despised. Only now are we beginning to recognise their gift for people, relationships, perception and emotion. These they are meant to discipline and then use in the world.

"Paul Tournier has called on women to use their own gifts,

because men have so controlled the world with their own gifts of reason and objectivity, that it is turning into a cold, objective, depersonalised machine, where people no longer matter. He calls on women to contribute what they have to give, and to be actively involved in society. Men and women in today's redeemed community should be demonstrating partnership in reconciliation. Man on his own was the only 'not good' part of creation.

"Churches need to be aware of the gifts women have, and mobilise them. Married women who have been caring for children may not be experienced in some areas, but they can learn, and every effort should be made to involve women in a meaningful contribution to the Church so that even when they are tied with young children, they do not lose touch with what is happening outside their homes.

"I feel that a lot of women need to be moving into positions of input on committees and in teams. Teams are Scriptural and women need to be on the same level as men, working alongside them. If they are then chosen for more of a leadership position, they are not usurping the position, but given it because of expertise and gift. It is often not easy to find women who are willing to work on teams and committees, because people are so often totally wrapped up in their homes locally. It is not Scriptural for either men or women to be running churches alone. I am beginning to find all-male leadership as objectionable as the thought of all-female leadership, because we are none of us infallible and we have been created to function together."

Sally McClung in conclusion says, "I have a firm conviction that God has created both men and women with the gifting and potential for leadership. It is individuals, structures and the norms of society which have held women back. Today women can do and be more than ever before. Women can be leaders of nations like Margaret Thatcher and Golda Meir. They can be astronauts or heads of business. There is a place for them in every aspect of society, but we in the Church can make it more complicated than it is meant to be. The gospel has freed women and where Christ has not been, women are still very downtrodden. Where there is the Spirit of Christ, there is freedom. God has given gifting into individual lives as He willed. Our responsibility is simply to be good stewards of what God has given us.

"There is still a lot of prejudice against women in leadership. We need to be careful that we do not dodge it and push our way through. We need rather to win our way through by serving, by loving, by forgiving and by having right, godly responses. We need to work at our leadership to make it more acceptable and be careful that we do not give emotional appeals, rather than good clear presentations. We need to avoid being confrontational, just because we are women. Neither must we take slights personally, but rather move into leadership clearly because of who we are and with the giftings we have.

"Because of prejudice women are sometimes judged more harshly than men would be. A quote from a section in a women's magazine recently said that we still do not talk about men and women in the same way. For instance, we say that a businessman is aggressive; but a businesswoman is pushy! He is careful about details; she is picky! He loses his temper, because he is so involved with his job; she cannot control her emotions. He is tenacious; she does not know when to quit. He is not afraid to say what he thinks; she is opinionated! He is a stern taskmaster; she is difficult to work for. In some instances, the man is still the one who makes more money than the woman, at the same job.

"I want to say that I am very grateful to be part of a missionary organisation that believes in women in leadership. It is a gift and privilege that has helped me develop and become who I am. I am also very grateful to have a husband who is so supportive. Floyd is known to be a real believer in and proponent of women in leadership.

"Being Floyd McClung's wife can sometimes open doors for me, but when I walk through those doors I have to have the goods, so to speak, or not go through! I cannot just coast on who my husband is. I am either a leader in my own right or I am not. If I am not, I have to find out what it is that God has for me. If I am, I must grow into all that God wants me to be. God has put it on my heart and called me into the area of teaching. There have been many times when men have challenged me as to why I am teaching, saying that it is unbiblical. I do not feel that is either a fair or true comment, but I have had to keep a right response and a gracious spirit in the midst of it.

"It is important to see that in the Bible the largest percentage of leaders are men, but there are certainly women leaders too. Dr. Cho, in Korea, says that women will do anything that men will release them to do. The stumbling block, I think, is where men have not brought release and opened the door for women. William Booth said that some of his best men were women. Floyd brought home a poster for me which was cute and so true. A woman is sitting over a cup of coffee, her glasses falling off her nose, looking worn and haggard. The quote below her says, 'They have found something that does the work of five men ... one woman!' We have overlooked the stamina and the strength of the female make-up. Child-bearing and child-raising require it. There is a real ability to endure within us, which is a blessing in leadership, because we do not give up easily.

"It is important that women moving into leadership do not imitate men, but that they are truly women. I have discussed this a lot with friends. One of the things that the single friends pointed out is that there are not enough women role-models. One of the most frustrating things for them, is that most of their models are men and they do not want to imitate men. I trust that as more women move into leadership, there will be more role-models to learn from. Women have taken major steps into leadership. Obviously they have made mistakes, but so have men. Women can be in positions of clear leadership. They are gifted for it with abilities and potential. The times are changing and we will see more and more women in leadership."

Finally, in our conclusions, in trying to find a solution to this issue and in hearing what the Holy Spirit is saying to the Church today, we first need to ask whether or not our enemy is at work in trying to deceive us in this whole area. Where emotions, feelings, insecurities, prejudice and tradition are concerned, he is often to be found at work. So this could be true particularly in the area of women in leadership.

A problem for some at this moment in time is in the area of governmental authority. Some men are not comfortable with women in authority. Some believe in ultimate male leadership of the Church (although not total male leadership), whilst endorsing a woman's pioneer ministry, like Jackie Pullinger. Others can easily see women apostles, which is a visionary work then passed on to local elders.

Some women too are not comfortable with a woman being an elder, even after having been involved in local leadership themselves. However, it may be that the personality involved is not comfortable in that sort of governmental position. It may be at the end of the day that some more subjective women would get too emotionally involved, and that eldership requires a greater objectivity in its office than some personalities allow for, whether male or female.

There is pain in moving into leadership. This develops qualities of character such as perseverance. For some it is too much and they opt for God's plan B, which can mean lots of children or taking another job. They can remain silent. However the joke has been that the woman who is silent in church rules at home! The pent-up frustration must come out somewhere. This is sometimes the flip side of the repressed gift. We deny the Church if we deny the gift, whoever it is in.

In Genesis we see that God's intention was that males and females were destined to have dominion or rule the earth together. Jesus commissioned us in Matthew 28:19-20 to go and tell the world about Him, making disciples, baptising and teaching them to obey His commandments, and He gave us His authority to do it. Christian men and women are coheirs with Jesus, seated with Him in heavenly places, in the place of authority.

We then have to ask why this is not fully worked out in church life today, and why so few women are involved? Paul had women striving at his side in the gospel, taking responsibility alongside him. So today, why is it not more of a feature of church life here? As an interesting side note, with the birth rate in England falling so drastically, there are going to be fewer male leaders anyway. If we are praying for an increase of His kingdom, what will we do if we refuse to recognise female leaders?

It seems that the main contentious verse is within 1 Timothy 2. In verse 12 we have the verse which talks about woman not having authority over a man. The word used in the Greek is *authentes*, which means 'to usurp authority' as opposed to *exousia*, which is the more normal Greek word used for authority elsewhere in the New Testament. In other words, Paul did not permit women to domineer over men, and until they had learned the correct attitude, they were to learn in silence. This was his own directive, as distinct from "Thus says the Lord". In 1 Timothy 3:3, the men too are told not to be quarrelsome!

So Paul's directive was that women were to learn to show themselves approved. Women who were only just beginning to read and write needed to be in the discipleship position. 2 Timothy 2:15 talks of those of whom God approves, correctly handling the word of truth. Firstly we learn a right attitude, then the word of truth and we also begin to hear God for ourselves. Thus the ability to be deceived is continuously being reduced, as we learn and move on in God and with one another. It is inevitable that as we mature we pass on to others what we have learnt. The new life within must find expression particularly in leadership, for those women and men with this gift of character. It cannot be denied.

The leadership that women seem to want most to be involved in is not a one-woman ministry. Just as single-parent families operate under a handicap, a Christian community under one-sex leadership is no different. The nature and heart of most women is to be in relationship, as part of the family and part of the team. Neither do they want to be women leaders who are just female men! Women want to be recognised for themselves and not, as in the past, by using their husband's name, an example of which would be Mrs Billy Graham.

So starting by following Jesus and becoming servants, we can fulfil our vocation as we follow the Lord who calls us. Then being motivated by hearing what God's heart is for each of us, we can become ready to move on towards our goal. Women in the Church are moving on. Some are beginning to travel towards being able to do whatever God is asking of them. The question then is whether the Church will encourage and make room for them to come to full maturity alongside the men, in both gift and function?

Leaders at their very best are doing themselves out of a job and moving over to give place to the next generation of leaders. Will the men in church leadership in this country be willing to give ground and place to the next generation of leaders, male and female, to move up alongside them? We will all one day be ruling and reigning in full measure. The restoration has to begin somewhere. Abroad is no longer good enough, for it appears that God is calling women leaders to serve Him today, in this country.

We must be fully convinced and strongly encourage it. As has been said elsewhere by my friend David Matthews, a well-known leader in the renewal: "Doing it, is doing it!" Can leaders today recognise those women as well as men who, like Moses, after many years have reached the point of saying, "I cannot do it, Lord," to whom God is now saying, "Yes, you can"?

In overcoming prejudice, tradition and insecurity, the attitude of present leaders is crucial, particularly their attitude to emerging women leaders. Scripture is very clear. In 1 Corinthians 11:11, we are told that woman is not independent of man nor is man independent of woman. Men and women need each other, to receive everything that comes from God. Neither will receive it alone. The operative word for the future must now be partnership.

Women have in past years laid down their ministry for the sake of their men and their children. Many have suppressed feelings for a long time. Coming out into new areas of leadership will mean some inner battles, such as overcoming the fear of man with the fear of the Lord. For some it may be too much, while others will have a go and flunk it, just as many men do. But still more will have a go and 'fly', if given the chance. Let the Holy Spirit move to join us together to build the kingdom where there are no wrong distinctions; neither Jew nor Greek, neither slave nor free, neither male nor female.

Ten

Women Apprenticing Leaders

Apprenticing means learning your craft. Down through history men have trained young men in work, very often a father his son. Sometimes a young man's hero will lead a man to train towards becoming like him. In both these examples, we see commitment and discipline. Women too have trained daughters in homemaking, and daughters too look for their heroes as models. Often today people follow heroes who are weak, living without commitment and responsibility. These 'heroes' exploit people, gaining power and are then cheered on. Heroes in the Bible are of a different order.

Jesus was a man to be followed and a man to learn from. He gave twelve men three years of His prime time. He lived with them and they learned day by day in real-life situations. There was no wrong intensity in this, but rather a bond established, whereby they could ask questions openly and be freely challenged, and probably challenge back as well. The security of their leader was not threatened at all.

Jesus had women travelling with Him as well as the twelve men (Luke 8:1-3). He did not freeze women out. His radical attitude paved the way for women to be right up front in the early Church too. Women were there as part of leadership teams, having meetings in their homes, and serving in every way possible. Younger Christians, both men and women, would have looked to them for example, encouragement and guidance.

To be a leader presupposes that you have people following you! Are women in leadership beginning to apprentice people in the Church and do they find they are able to make disciples of others in the area of their gift? How have women in leadership in the Church today begun to move in this area? What has the Holy Spirit said to them about leading those people who are following after them?

Pat Cook begins by sharing how she is actively leading a team of missionaries. "Originally I was the leader and they just followed. I kept control and was the boss and they had very little opportunity to have input. It was a bit like a managing director of a business firm. Now my leadership position has changed. I am a leader of far more people, and I now lead from behind, by serving and by example. Finding what jobs are not done, I will turn and do them myself and serve the team. If I want my missionaries to be servants, I serve them. If someone has a gift, I will try and see that it is developed and used, to complement the whole team.

"In recognising each person's gifts and weaknesses, I want to see all the team members fully developed. It is like a shepherd with a flock of sheep — they recognise the personalities and the individual idiosyncrasies and weaknesses. I do not feel a leader needs to be leading all the time; we just need to be in control, unobtrusively, and delegate, encouraging others out into their own field and ability. In West Asia there is a lot of fear and you lead by example. It also depends on who your team is as to how you lead it. Sometimes you have to be strong, whereas in our office now, you might occasionally wonder who is leading! The key is to lead by example, which has a price!"

People by nature are influenced by role-models. So they are affected by the kind of people leaders are and by the kind of way they live, rather than by their words alone. As they test themselves against such models, God is more interested in who leaders are, than in what they do. We need to get hold of the fact that God is making us the people He wants us to be, not so we can rush around and do jobs everywhere, but rather in order that we can glorify Him and worship Him better.

Sally McClung has also worked in Asia and shares that she has learned to lead those following after her, as she would want to be led herself. She continues, "I am very aware that in this mission, I am a role-model, both in terms of my own leadership through the years and also in terms of being Floyd's wife. Many people have looked upon me as an example and that is awesome. I do not take it lightly. So I have tried to be a woman leader that I would feel comfortable under and that I would want to follow. There are a number of aspects included in this, which I have tried to incorporate into my leadership and life.

"One is servanthood. You are not a leader in order to be served, but rather to serve. I try to serve those that I lead spiritually and practically. I have missed opportunities, and not always made it, but I have endeavoured to serve those for whom I have responsibility. I have also tried to release those under me, as I am very grateful to those over me who have released me into areas of responsibility. I want to help others to find their area of gifting and ministry, where they will find their fulfilment. I also try to be an encourager. This ministry is sorely lacking in the Body of Christ. We do not affirm and build up one another enough. I want to praise, support and help, because I appreciate it myself when people do it to me.

"I have tried to be a leader who leads in the fear of God. There have been times when I have missed it and feared man. But as I grow and mature, I am more sensitive to lead with the fear of God upon me. I have also tried to lead in obedience to the new steps and challenges that God has had for me. As a woman, having found a place of leadership, there is a temptation to rest in that place, to find security in it and dig in and stay there. This has not been the way the Lord has led me. There have been new steps and challenges for me to grow and develop. My responsibilities have multiplied many times through the years.

"I have also tried to lead in the more feminine aspects of being gentle, gracious, open, warm and loving. I have needed to grow in some of these areas. I have tried to be who I am in the areas of my strength and also be feminine along with it, rather than taking on the more masculine characteristics

of leadership. The area of dress is important. Women moving
into the area of leadership sometimes become more masculine
in order to look more important or to be seen as leaders. This
is a mistake. There are some styles that have a masculine
quality to them that are OK for women, for instance slacks.
I wear them a lot, because it fits my life style in the city.
However, I dress in my slacks in a feminine way. We must
not pick up a form of dress that looks masculine, in order
to be more acceptable.

"It is important to be continually growing. My personal
walk with the Lord must not stagnate. I need something fresh
and new to lead with and give out to those who are following
me. We also need to realise that leadership involves pressure,
particularly for a woman, when trying to combine home,
family and ministry or career. I teach on burnout and stress
management. There are simple, practical, godly principles
that we can live by that will help us. Sometimes I say that
the pressures I face today would probably have put me in
hospital with a nervous breakdown five or ten years ago.
However, our pressure quotient can be stretched and
expanded. One of my prayers is that God will expand me
and help me to be able to take more and more responsibility
and leadership, in order to be more effective for the kingdom
of God. Women also need to know if they need to cut back.
We must find out what our priorities are, and what our right
responses and choices are in the face of pressure."

Patricia Higton explains that as a woman in leadership, she
is aware that she expects a lot from people. "Because God
has enabled me to respond by His grace to the challenge to
serve Him, and I want to do it with everything I have got,
I expect other people to do the same. So I tend to challenge
people to the depth of their being. If people make excuses
of inferiority or fear, I try to help them overcome these and
not hide behind them. I can help people from my own
experience in relation to fear, which has been quite a
dominant factor in my own life.

"In leading others I also throw them in at the deep end!
I delegate and observe from a distance, by letting them make
mistakes. I find that people grow this way and discover their

own potential, or rather what God has given them. I remember delegating the whole of the prayer ministry in the parish, where we have twenty or so prayer cells, to one of our ladies. There was no way she wanted to do that at all, or felt she was capable of it, so with somewhat less than gentle persuasion, I encouraged her to do it. She has in fact proved to be better at it than I ever was, and it was the right thing for her.

"I feel there will always be a category of people who will not respond to that kind of leadership. They tend to be those who are hanging on to various areas of their life that they don't want to let go. They are trying to protect themselves, afraid to take risks or steps of faith. I would tend to hand that kind of person over to someone with pastoral gifts to help them. But I do find that both men and women often respond to a challenge, if their hearts are basically set to follow God."

Leaders often have a problem of impatience with those who have not seen what the next step should be. Leadership frustration can almost rage at times, waiting for people to catch up, even months or years later. No one is perfect. Whether a leader feels good or bad at times is not the issue. A leader just needs to get on and lead as God has called.

Eileen Vincent feels that she has been something of a trailblazer and a pioneer in many areas. "I know I have moulded women's ideas, particularly those who have been closely involved with me. I have taught on women's ministry and the place of women in the Church, so in that respect I guess I have led. I have also endeavoured to lead people to understand the bigness of their salvation, and to deal with the smallness of their own attitudes. I run our annual women's weekend, and we used to have a very effective women's work, but as the work has grown we've cut back more and more. Since the bringing in of house-groups such things are covered in other ways.

"I also teach when I am abroad, particularly to women. I think the fact that you are in leadership means that even if you don't say anything, something still shows to other people. Alan and I have always been pioneers, and were in the forefront of many of the attitudes on women today. The paper Alan wrote, many years ago, is only now beginning to be talked about. It contains such things as that a woman is really free in the Church to do anything, except lead the whole shooting match!''

Marion White does not feel that she is in a specific leadership role, on a paid basis. She explains, ''I know that I am a leader because people follow me, especially the Youth for Christ staff, wives as well as other people that I come into contact with. Anyone who speaks at all will find people looking up to them. But the thing I want to get across most to people is the way that men and women have complementary roles, and the way we can be used powerfully together.

''Rob and I speak a lot on the family and on relationships, husbands and wives and children. We run an engaged couples' weekend. In this way I am involved practically in leading people. What I don't want to come across is that I just want to be a dominant woman who loves being a leader and having a following. I want it to be something that really brings glory to God, is powerful and effective in the Church, and actually says something.

''Another way I lead is in one-to-one contact, which is valuable particularly for younger women. I have also done specific teaching on Women In Ministry, and on women's roles. Last year I did a ladies' weekend for Youth for Christ. It was for all the wives, staff and associates of YFC, and it was to encourage the women to enter into the gifts and abilities God has given them and then branch out. I took some of the younger women, in whom I could see gifts, and gave them a slight push into doing a speaking role. We also had music, dance, drama, worship and it was tremendously encouraging to me to see them step out.

''When I first came into YFC, the women were rather forgotten, not being invited to meetings and being left looking after the children. Rob and I worked to involve whole families. God gave me a picture of a map of Great Britain. Across it there were rows and rows of women standing. They all had their heads bowed. Then there was a lovely picture of Jesus walking down every row, and as He came to every woman He stopped and just put His hand under her chin and raised her head. I just felt that this is what I want to see in this nation.''

Some leaders can inhibit people and make them feel inferior. Good leaders enable people to voice their views, or join in a conversation, which can be very constructive. It sharpens young minds, and the tension is creative. Because the gifts of God are found scattered between the sexes, each person is a unique gift in themselves. It is obvious that a leader, by definition, can recognise gift or ability as it develops in another man or woman. Recognising some people's gifts and getting them into positions where they can launch into using these gifts for the good of the whole Church has been done by some women in leadership. They have been able to do this for men and women, opening doors for them because of the positions they hold.

General Eva Burrows says, ''Concerning those who are following me, I do not lead from a long way ahead. Our relationships are very personal and everyone relates to me as the head of the family, so that there is affection, as well as a respect. I would like to feel that they follow me with that motivation.''

Sue Barnett is in a very interesting position now. Having been involved in the leadership of the Saltmine Trust for a year, she has found it necessary gradually to withdraw from leadership in her home group, both in the church and in the town where she lives. She continues, ''I have had good training in this area of apprenticing, because I have had to think very carefully about training those who are following after me. A vital area of leadership is encouraging the gift in others and training people to fill our positions in the future. Saltmine has a two-year training scheme with young people developing their gifts in drama, music and preaching, to become more effective in sharing their faith.

''Relationships are very important and are the key to

leadership. Being in close prayerful relationship in the team results in everything else becoming a natural outworking of that, both within the work as well as outside in evangelism. So in my initial preparation, I find people to lead with me as well as follow after me. It is important to have relationships outside the work, so there is an all-round depth of commitment that leads to trust and security.

"There is a limit to how many we can be close to. Jesus had just twelve disciples. The person who has taken over from me in leadership is my closest friend. She has been widowed and is now a single person in leadership. We leaders need to move on, in God's time, so that others can grow, and that is what has happened here. There is something wrong with a person's leadership if the work falls apart after they have left. Some feel that it is a compliment, but I don't think that is what God wants at all.

"I have been involved in leadership in an outreach down in Bournemouth that packs the Pavilion with people from the neighbourhood and involves lots of churches. I don't just chair the committee, but have a network of hostesses throughout the area. One of the biggest needs is mutual encouragement and praying together. The outreach lunch in Bournemouth had an initial committee of eight who made the decisions. We had a wider team of fifty hostesses, and worked with the Pavilion staff. My first job was to be working with all these people, in training and encouraging. Trust is so important. Breakdown can happen here first of all. The leader must be the cog on which everything else turns, so that when unpopular decisions are made, the strong network of relationships stays with you."

Some women and their husbands are too busy to lead in the more conventional ways, such as in partnership, leading a house-group. If leadership is apparent in the character, then an active asking about the concerns of that person can open up or even pioneer a whole new area for the Church. Daytime activities can begin, or new forums can be set up to preach the gospel and build the Church. There are many different ways to lead and some are unusual.

Jean Darnall is not aware that anyone is following in her footsteps! She tells us, ''Even my daughter is very much her own self. I don't think she aspires to be anything like me. I just preach the gospel and minister to people and they follow the Lord. When I teach in the college, I'm not there all the time like Elmer. The students are very much his students. I teach a subject and then move on, so I am not in a sense making disciples of people, and I seldom work in teams. When I've pastored in the past, we've led the congregation by counselling and visiting as well as preaching. I can still recognise gifts and ministries and encourage them and speak to them, often prophetically. This is a gift that the Lord has given me.

''When I do join a team, it is something like a pastoral team or YWAM, and I am there for a short season, ministering in a transient way. I've not had that concept of people belonging to my ministry in any way. I'm in a different situation from a woman who is working in a pastoral role. I am travelling all the time; in a few months I travel to Holland, Hawaii, the US, Norway, Denmark and Belgium! My ministry does not allow much time for strong interpersonal relationships. I suppose that is a weakness, if there is one in my ministry. It may be that I don't have that ability, or the inclination to work in a team in a situation. My husband and I are very interdependent and communicate very closely and we are a team together.''

Rosemary Andrews explains that she and Ian help people in the healing ministry, by keeping in touch with those they teach. She continues, ''We get them to give us feedback and encourage them to move on further into what God has for them. We also lead others by going on ahead, by example and by teaching. We let them sit with us and learn by seeing us do it and then they go and put it into practice in their own lives. People can come back to us again in group situations, because we are available.''

Women have got to be given the chance to make mistakes, just as men have been. There is nothing dreadful about it. It is part of much of the learning process. The perfectionist slant of the teaching from the past has made it such a serious thing to make a mistake that far too much weight has been given to it. It then becomes a really heavy thing to apologise. It should be an easy thing to say that we are sorry, and then to get on and not make the same mistake again.

Bren Robson knows that training and apprenticing are vital. She says, "I have found it very important to have faith in the Holy Spirit in people. This has helped me to risk it and allow people to learn from their own mistakes. For those that I apprentice, I do what I can to be with them in their difficulties. Sometimes it is hard not to rescue people, but God has to do His own work of refining, and a rescue job would be, on some occasions, working against the Holy Spirit's work in someone's life.

"Right from the start of any appointment in the Church, I suggest that the person concerned should be thinking about who is coming next after them: I hope I have led by example, encouragement, personal contact, steering, and when necessary giving direction, rather than good advice. It is so easy to want to give good advice, but so much more important for people to make their own decisions and take their own risks.

"Getting together regularly, making assessments and goal setting are also vital. People need to feel fulfilled and that they have achieved something. I want to find servant hearts, people who are willing to follow and people who are teachable. I try to provide opportunities for those following me, taking them with me on trips. Perhaps most important of all, I share with them my own struggles, and try to be vulnerable with them. I don't want to remain aloof, and by sharing my own weakness, I find that they realise that I am human, just as they are. I find that people are then more ready to trust. Sometimes of course it is important to point out areas of personal life which need attention, but more often than not, these are voluntarily shared.

"In bringing any issue into church life, in the Guildford Community Church we usually deliberately avoid that which is contrary to the emphasis we are trying to bring. This has been true for the last five years in establishing that women as well as men can be free to minister and lead, if that is their calling. Therefore, we have deliberately avoided men-only meetings or women-only meetings, because we are trying to pioneer in this area of bringing men and women together.''

Grace Barnes shares that when she started out, she had a small women's fellowship of four to six women, although she had no training and had never been to Bible College. ''God showed me clearly to work with what I had, because He was going to use women. So I did. I gave them tea, did their washing and ironing and whatever was needed. Gradually new converts came in like Chris Norton, who is now one of our leaders, and things began to grow.

''At the beginning we decided to work ourselves out of a job, and give it away. For me this meant taking Chris Norton with me everywhere I went. She was our first young woman convert. I served her, as she served me. We do need more encouragement in the Church, when people do things well.

''The next development was like a revelation to me. If God was going to use women in ministries, they needed to know how to minister in big halls, and how to handle and use a microphone. So I encouraged our girls to take the meetings, give testimonies, or lead a chorus. I felt God was saying that we were to get prepared for when the door would be opened. I am proud to say now that there are girls around me who are far more able to speak than I am. This is how it should be, because every generation should be taught and then learn from God, and so become better than the generation before them.

''So it has cost me in time, in loving, caring, teaching, and encouraging them. I have opened up doors, and then stepped down and let them come up in front. We don't want women in leadership for the sake of it. If they are not there functioning, we don't want a woman just sitting in, to prove we have a woman in leadership! They must be there on a real basis, gifted for the job, with the right qualities, capable of doing it well.''

Women coming into leadership will bring a new aspect to it. They often find it difficult to understand how men have talked about leadership in the past in such a definitive way. Perhaps that was just the slant of male leadership. Also women do not seem to need so much recognition, not that they should not be recognised, but they have learned to cope with the lack of it.

True servant leadership rubs off on people. You can leave people in fear if you leave them with too much room to manoeuvre too soon. Some people like it, but others panic. It is often uncomfortable at first being up front. People moving into leadership must be prepared to take a higher profile role. Knowing that a servant leader is there to help fill the gap expands a person until eventually the mind grasps and remembers how to do the job effectively. We need this principle outworked in families for our children as well.

Christine Noble concludes for us. ''I want to feel I have led those following me by being who I am, by being an example and by blazing some sort of trail, sometimes through a jungle place where no one has been before, making it easier for those coming up behind me. I feel I have led by being willing to be wrong, living dangerously and being open to criticism, often from people who neither appreciate nor understand my gift in God, and also by not covering up when I fail. My leading has been amongst both men and women. I feel I have a mother's heart and am more anxious to see children doing things than doing things myself. I can encourage folk into the things they are good at. A real mother is not threatened by the fact that her children will soon overtake her.

''A mother has sons and daughters and she does not just encourage her daughters, any more than a father just encourages his sons. For example, I have taken one of my natural sons into a counselling session as an observer. When he seemed confident, I suggested to him that he should pray to set the person free from the spirits which had been named. That gave him the security to know that he could handle that kind of situation. I have also taken men as well as women counsellors to work alongside me at conferences and meetings. I made it clear that I would stand with them, whilst they set people free for themselves, and so they have begun to move in ministry."

So we begin to draw our final conclusions. Jesus said, "Go and make disciples." He had men and women following Him, so the assumption is that they were to go further into the world of men and women, and see them converted, trained and matured in a manner similar to the way Jesus had trained them. Today, in the Church, there is sometimes a danger of heavy shepherding, where it seems that people need to ask permission to do anything! Wrong ideas of authority and submission are often more to do with fearful and insecure leaders than true making of disciples.

Jesus won people's hearts and minds by who He was. He did not function with a set of rules. He consistently wanted people to function in the way that He did, hearing from God and 'risking it' again and again. He wanted people to learn to live under grace, not under law. He allowed His disciples to make mistakes, and then talked to them about where they had gone wrong, before encouraging them to go on again. Above everything else, they knew that they were apprenticed to someone who cared.

Women, who have been so unused to leading, need to learn and train alongside men, so that together they can begin to have dominion. Adam needed Eve. Men in leadership must make room for women leaders. Sometimes a woman can be in leadership with her husband, if that is her gift; at other times a married or single woman will have the gift of leadership on her own, and can work as part of a team. There is so much to learn. We need to understand the nature of leadership and executive ability. Total spontaneity will not build the kingdom of God. The right kind of strategic planning is always needed. Room needs to be made for women to move into their level of gift, whether leading a small group or leading a community of people or training other men and women in leadership.

So often the elders and deacons are men who are sent off for training without the women. There is a real need for women not to be left out. If women in the Church today are going to move into leadership, they need training and apprenticing for this. Just as Mary sat at Jesus' feet in the discipleship position, so women today need this kind of facility. Leadership training needs to be opened up to women of ability, whether married or single, black or white.

It has been said that women as well as men must use their minds and personalities and experience at leadership level, or we are not going to be able to cope with the next set of liberal theologians. Women who teach do so on the same basis as any man: on the basis of the authority of the Word of God, and they should be tested by that. Today in many Christian circles there is an emphasis on experience. But our future teachers and college lecturers, etc. are always going to be people who have more than just a basic qualification, and have gone into research. Often women do not have doctorates and further degrees to open up such fields of leadership. These things need to be considered.

It is the mark of a leader to have people following. Women in leadership, as we have seen, are beginning to pioneer training and apprenticing in this area of team ministry. They are challenging people, serving, being vulnerable, delegating, using their minds and feelings and risking it, preparing for the next generation by organic growth.

A mixture of administrative and prophetic gift is beginning to flow; logical people are moving with intuitive people, women included, to organise meetings and network across the different streams and denominations. But there is more to do yet. The further you move into church leadership the more people-orientated you must become, a gift women leaders can excel in. In some Asian countries, where church growth is so fast, whole areas of leadership are being given to women.

For us, today, I believe God's heart is for women and men to move together in partnership and team leadership, training other men and women together, in order to see worldwide church growth and the evangelisation of every tribe and nation in our generation, in order to bring back the King. May God give each of us grace to be able to respond and play our part in this, at whatever level of leadership we find ourselves, whether men or women.

Conclusion
by
Dave Tomlinson

Women in Church Leadership

Introduction: Interpreting Scripture

Interpreting the Bible is far from easy. Those who argue that Scripture is readily understandable by anyone are naive and run the danger of encouraging its abuse. Knowing God on a personal level doesn't require any intellectual qualification, and spiritual insight is not dependent on theological agility, but these issues are distant from the proper handling and interpretation of the Bible.

Throughout history, basic rules of interpretation have been recognised and practised. They cannot guarantee correct conclusions regarding particular passages, but they should always be applied when we are seeking to understand Scripture aright.

What are these principles?

1. Always interpret a verse in agreement with its context. The meaning of one part should be consistent with the whole.
2. Interpret a passage in the light of its probable meaning to the persons to whom it was originally written.
3. Take into account the customs and events of the period when it was written.
4. Interpret a passage in the light of the rest of Scripture.
5. Do not use an obscure passage to disprove one clear, obvious meaning.

6. Interpret a passage according to the best use of the original language.
7. Interpret social teaching in line with doctrinal teaching.
8. If there is a principle set forth in the passage, do not interpret or apply the passage in such a way as to deny or reverse the principle.
9. Interpret the unknown in accordance with the known.
10. Do not interpret a passage in such a way as to make it deny what we know to be true of God from other Scripture.

Historical background is obviously a key factor in dealing with the issue of women, since the status of women in Greek, Roman, and Jewish cultures in New Testament times was very different to that of today in our own society.

> Individual texts must be carefully analysed and the conditions of the times which gave rise to particular statements or formed their background must be borne in mind. Any interpretation which is not controlled by the historical context of the passage misinterprets the Bible. [1]

In fact many passages and practices in the New Testament are automatically interpreted in the light of their historical context rather than being taken literally. We barely notice the fact until some controversy arises relating to such passages.

For example:

- The practice of footwashing. (John 13:14)
- The prohibition of eating blood in any form. (Acts 15:29)
- Paul's advocacy of celibacy. (1 Corinthians 7:8,27)
- Paul's apparent condoning of, or at least failure to openly condemn, the practice of slavery. As with the women issue, he seemed to stress a higher priority — that of preserving the testimony, and avoiding unnecessary persecution — at that time. (1 Corinthians 7:21-23)
- Terms used in Jesus' ministry such as:
    'going an extra mile'
    'the eye of a needle'
  each of which had very specific local and historical meaning.

The Overall Picture

This paper is arguing that women are biblically qualified to serve as elders or leaders in the Church.

I believe there to be a unity and consistency in Scripture which can be recognised once we have rid ourselves of preconceived notions and interpretations of the meaning of particular passages.

My argument will be to show:

a) That women were made equally in the image of God with men and only in full partnership can they express that image, and that both women and men were given God's commission to 'rule over' the natural creation.

b) That through the Fall a 'battle of the sexes' was begun which God foretold would lead to female subjugation, and that this was not His will, but His prophecy as to the consequences of the Fall.

c) That the message of the new covenant is one of liberation, restoring to women the potential to recover their true and full equality.

d) That Jesus demonstrated this 'good news' to women in His actions.

e) That Paul argued consistently for the acceptance of women as full equals on the basis of their partnership in creation and laid the foundation for their participation at every level of leadership.

f) That cultural and historical reasons for the slowing down of the process of liberation in the first century were not binding throughout history.

Following or Leading the World?

Those who advocate the liberation of women in the Church are sometimes accused of 'following the world', i.e. the feminists.

The danger of the Church having its agenda formed by its social environment is a real one, but in this instance I would like to make two observations.

Firstly, modern feminism is actually predated by Christian

or biblical feminism. The present feminist movement burs
onto the scene in 1967 with the women's liberatio
demonstration at the Miss America competition in Atlanti
City, NJ. Most of the recent developments in terms of th
legislation as well as changes in attitude have sprung out c
the Atlantic City outburst. Prior to this, of course, there wa
the Suffragette movement at the beginning of this century

Whilst secular feminists look back to the Enlightenment fo
their roots, Christian feminists would argue that women'
rights were placed on the social agenda in a large measur
by Christians.

Even in the Reformation period moves were under way t
improve the lot of women. Luther and Calvin, who are hardl
known as feminists, refuted the Catholic notion of wome
being unclean tools of the devil. Divorce on the grounds o
proven adultery was obtainable for women as well as mer
a reform only placed on the English statute books in 1923

In Puritan homes girls were frequently educated alongsid
their brothers and even studied theology. Groups like th
Quakers gave full rights for women to preach and teach a
early as the 17th century.

But biblical feminism came into its own in the 19th century
The cause was often championed alongside anti-slavery
temperance and legislation to protect prostitutes. Th
Salvation Army has had total equality as part of it
constitution since its inception, and documents by Catherine
Booth, in which she argues for the full rights of women, ar
still available.

Biblical feminist activity provided much of the spade wor
which prepared the way for the Suffragettes. It is interesting
to note that many of the agruments put forward today t
inhibit the emancipation of women in the Church are th
same as those offered to oppose women having the vote.

Secondly, I have to ask why it is assumed that the worl
is wrong? In reality, we all 'follow the world' in lots of ways
if this were not the case we would be forced to drop out o
society. We thankfully receive the world's wisdom (no
uncritically) in terms of culture and technology as well a
presuppositions. In the Hebrew Scriptures we read of Goc
speaking through heathen kings, to say nothing of an ass

Unfortunately, we evangelicals have allowed our doctrine of the Fall to obliterate our doctrine of Creation. God's image is still reflected in mankind and is expressed creatively, relationally and ethnically as well as in wisdom and knowledge.

Genesis 1:26-28

Two points are indisputable from this passage:

a) that women share equally in the image of God with men, and

b) that women were given an equal share in the mandate to rule in God's creation. So let's look at these points.

a) Women share in God's image

The traditional assumption is that God, insofar as He can be defined in sexual terms, is an exclusively male deity and that this gives obvious foundation for the policy of men, not women, exercising leadership and authority (particularly in the Church).

Whilst it's true that God is revealed mostly in masculine terms in the Bible, it's by no means exclusively the case. For example:

Psalm 123:2	master and mistress
Psalm 131:2	loving mother
Isaiah 49:13-15	" "
Isaiah 66:13	" "
Psalm 22:9	a midwife
Isaiah 42:14	a pregnant woman

The Hebrew noun *reham* (womb) in the plural form *rah mim* becomes an abstraction translated 'love', 'compassion' or 'mercy'. ''The biblical idea of Yahweh as a merciful and compassionate Being draws its strength from feminine symbolism and carried maternal overtones, although the usual translators are insensitive to this. (cf. Deuteronomy 4:31; Isaiah 49:13,15)''[2]

Sometimes feminine nouns are used to describe aspects of God's person or character, but they usually pass unnoticed. For example, the righteousness of God appears in both masculine (*sedak*) and feminine (*sdakah*) forms. Again the

Hebrew term for the 'Spirit', 'wind', 'breath' of God is feminine (*ruah*). The Hebrew word for God's law (*torah*) is feminine. The 'wisdom' of God (*hokmah*) of which the Greek word *logos* (as in John 1:1 etc.) is an extension, appears not only in the grammatical sense as feminine, but it is also depicted as a woman (Proverbs 7:4).[3]

El Shaddai, one of God's names, is of feminine source meaning the 'breasted one' (the Hebrew word *shad* means breast) usually translated 'all-sufficient one'.

Similar observations could be made in the New Testament. For example, New Testament writers choose to use the word *anthropos* (human being) when describing Jesus, rather than *aner* which specifically means male. In the book of Revelation the glorified Jesus is protrayed as having female breasts though modern translators obscure the fact. (The AV translated it 'paps' as in Luke 11:27; 23:29.) But whilst they establish clearly the non-exclusivity of masculine images of God, they do little to prove anything regarding the sexuality of God. Whilst being the source of all that is good in what we call masculine and feminine, God surely transcends sexual definition.

Most theologians would agree with this but sadly, "They have hardly been consistent in applying this truth. Whilst they have assumed that God is not female, it has been less clear to them that He is not male either."[4]

Symbolic and anthropomorphic language is a mere accommodation to human speech and understanding. The full projection of God's image in human terms can only be expressed through the unity, equality and complementarity of the sexes.

b) Joint responsibility in 'ruling'

Little need be said on this point beyond a straightforward observation of the fact. Those who argue that 'rule' is an inappropriate task for women to fulfil fail to see how things were in the beginning. Absolutely no prescription of roles is mentioned in Genesis chapter 1. We can only assume that they were to do the job on the basis of individual gifts and talents. The key is that they were to rule together, not on an individual or rota basis. "Man is created neither unisex (male or female), nor androgynous (male and female in one person) but with sexual duality as male and female.''[5]

Genesis 2:18-25

Three arguments are drawn from this passage to establish that women should be subject to men in terms of authority and function.
a) Man was created first.
b) Woman was made from man.
c) Woman was given as a 'helper' to man.
If we were to divest ourselves of preconceptions, the first two points offer no logic whatsoever.

In the chapter 1 account of creation, man is actually made last of all, following the earth, the heavens and all living creatures. Does the argument of priority out of chronological order mean that man should be subject to the creatures? Surely, man was made last as the crowning glory of creation, so by reverse chronology, woman should be supreme!

Should women be subject to men on the grounds of Eve being created from Adam? Again, what logic lies behind such an argument? Adam was made from the dust of the earth — does this suggest that men should be subject to the earth?

> No indication of female subordination is contained in the use of the word *issa* (taken out of), it is simply a Hebrew figure of speech. *Issa* is 'taken out of', but so is Adam 'taken out of' *damah* (earth) and Adam is not portrayed as a supernumerary addition to the earth, nor as a subordinate to it.[6]

The real point behind both of these facts is that women
a) have an equal stake in creation — they were made by God too, and
b) they were made of the same substance as men — nothing inferior or superior.
How much better the world would be if we could really believe these truths.

The 'helpmeet' argument appears at face value to have more substance, until we look a little closer.

The word *ezer* is badly translated as 'helpmeet' or 'helpmate'. There is certainly nothing in the word itself to suggest subservience. In fact, out of the nineteen times it is used in the Hebrew Scripture, fifteen of them refer to God being a 'help' to His people (e.g. Genesis 49:25; Exodus 18:4; Deuteronomy 33:26). Probably the most familiar passage is in 1 Samuel 7:12 where Samuel sets up a memorial stone and calls it 'stone of help' or Ebenezer, because, "hitherto the Lord has helped us."

"A helper fit for him has the force of 'equal and adequate to'. There is no hint of inferiority; woman is not man's subordinate, but stands in her integrity by his side before God."[7]

Partnership is the sense of this verse; complimentarity and completion. This is borne out of the fact that man was 'not good' alone but needed another corresponding half.

In What Way Did Things Change After The Fall?

Genesis 3:16

This verse is often used as a statement of 'Divine Order'. Not at all. It comes after the Fall and is God's prophecy as to the consequences of the Fall, not as a declaration of His will or purpose. Some argue that, even though this be the case, we should accept it since we do live in a fallen world. If this be the case, for consistency, we would need to shun labour-saving devices, underarm deodorant and prayer for the sick, to say nothing of the whole of medicine. God went on to speak of the 'seed of the woman' who would bruise the serpent's head.

"Your desire shall be to your husband", has been interpreted as being a sexual desire by many commentators and translators. This view seems to stem from an Italian Dominical monk, called Pagnino, who actually translated the word 'lust' when he published his translation of the Hebrew Bible in the 16th century. Every English translation since has tended to give the word that meaning but all the ancient translations render it as 'turning' or 'will turn to'. The root of the word *teshuga* is 'to run'. Used as it is in this case in its intensive form it could be rendered 'to run back and forth', or 'to turn frequently'. Hence it would read, "You are continually turning to your husband and he will rule over you." Bushnell concludes that Eve would be turning *away* from God *to* her husband and consequently her dependence would lead to Adam ruling over her.[8]

"Neither Male nor Female in Christ"

Galatians 3:28

There is a break in the symmetry of the three pairs, in the Greek, when 'and' is placed between the last pair (male AND female), as in the Revised Version, rather than 'nor', as in other versions. It is likely that Paul was here alluding to Genesis 1:27. It certainly could not be advocating any kind of androgyny (obliteration of sexes). Bruce maintains that distinctions between the groups remain — it's the *values* and *roles* which are destroyed.[9]

The context is Paul's concern regarding the law and the new covenant. "The three pairs in verse 28 highlight three fundamental areas of inequality manifested in the law, where Gentiles, slaves and women were at best third-class citizens, at worst 'non-persons'."[10] Caird comments, "The one thing these three pairs have in common is that they denote the three deepest divisions which split society in the ancient world. What Paul is saying is that such divisions can have no place in the thought of those who are united with Christ."[11]

Paul's concern was that in Christ the effects of the Fall, embodied in the law and expressed through patriarchal Jewish culture, were abrogated. Women, like slaves and Gentiles, are received into full membership of the kingdom of God, restored to their creational freedom.

Herein lies the essential harmony between the various Pauline statements on the subject. In spite of the superficial differences between 1 Corinthians 11:2-16 and Galatians 3:26f, Paul's deepest thoughts on male-female relations and women's status are the same in both passages. In both he strives to convey the truth that 'in the Lord' (1 Corinthians 11:11), 'in Christ' (Galatians 3:28) men and women are equal and independent. Neither sex is more privileged than the other, neither is bound in subjection to the other, together they are released from past restrictions to worship and serve God freely and responsibly. [12]

Several commentators agree that Galatians 3:27-28 represented a pre-Pauline liturgical formula for baptism. If this be the case, it provides us not only with a statement of Paul's position but with an insight into the theological understanding of the early Church as a whole. [13] The early Christians understood themselves as freed by the Holy Spirit to a new life of egalitarian discipleship. "Over the patriarchal patterns of 'the world' over against the commonly accepted ratification of sexual discrimination in Judaism and Hellenism, they set up the equality and freedom of the children of God." [14]

What is the Meaning and Application of Headship?

1 Corinthians 11:2-16

This is arguably one of the most crucial and also the most complicated passages relating to the role of women. Let's just outline the main issues:
a)   What is the meaning of the word 'head' in verse 3?
b)   Does verse 3 constitute a hierarchy or 'chain of command'?
c)   What is meant by 'power' or 'authority' on a woman's head? (verse 10)
d)   What is the sense of the 'headcovering' issue?
e)   What is the overall message of the passage?
  Let's begin with two observations on this passage:
1.   That no one can confidently claim to understand all the intricacies of Paul's arguments, especially as they relate to local custom, and
2.   That his meaning was probably quite obvious to the original readers.

We are dealing with statements drenched with local significance and there is therefore a distinct danger that we will misread or misunderstand what is actually being said. Building doctrines on passages with obscure meanings is recognised to be a hazardous exercise.

Let's take up some of the key issues.

a) The meaning of the word 'head'

What is a true definition of the word 'head' (*kephale*)? Out of the fifty-seven times it is used in the New Testament, fifty of them simply refer to the head of a person or animal. The other seven use the word metaphorically, which is where the difficulty lies. Two of them have been interpreted as meaning 'having authority', both of them relating to men and women (1 Corinthians 11:3; Ephesians 5:23).

Since there is no intrinsic meaning of authority in the word 'head', it's necessary to understand how it would have been used metaphorically in Paul's day. *We* use it to describe a chief, boss or leader e.g. 'head of an organisation'; there seems little evidence that Paul would have used it that way.

To begin with, there is a physiological complication: almost all authorities agree that the heart was considered the source of thought and emotion, whereas the head was the source of life. Palmer's Bible Dictionary states, "The head is not regarded as the seat of.the intellect, but as the source of life ... thus to lift the head is to grant life in the sense of success".[15] The New Bible Dictionary says, "The head is not regarded as the seat of the intellect, but the source of life", and it goes on to say:

> When Christ is spoken of as the head of His body, the Church (Ephesians 5:23; Colossians 2:19), of every man (1 Corinthians 11:3), of the entire universe (*hyperpanta*, Ephesians 1:22), and of every cosmic power (Colossians 2:10), and when man is spoken of as the head of the woman (1 Corinthians 11:3; Ephesians 5:23; cf. Genesis 2:21f), the basic meaning of head as the source of all life and energy is predominant. Hence to interpose allegiance to any other spiritual mediator, as was being done at

Colossae, severs the vital connection between the limbs and Christ the head, the mainspring of all spiritual energy. [16]

S. Bedale who has written a whole book on the subject of verse 3 based on the meaning of *kephale* affirms clearly that 'source' is the true rendering in pre-biblical Greek, not 'superior rank'. [17] The correctness of this would seem to be confirmed by comparing verse 3 with verse 8 (RSV) — ''For man was not made from woman, but woman from man'' — which re-emphasises that woman was derived from man.

Barratt argues that verse 3 refers to the *origin* of woman on the basis that Paul could have used an obvious alternative such as *kurios* (lord), if he'd meant to convey the idea of *rank*. [18]

By far the most obvious rendering of the word 'head' in the metaphorical sense is 'source' or 'origin' as in the 'head of a river'.

b) Verse 3 — a hierarchy?

What of verse 3 as a whole; does it lay out a chain of command or hierarchy — God, Christ, Man, Woman? This idea is undermined in that we have to rearrange the components to make it look that way. As it stands, it reads — Christ, Man, Woman, God. What we have in this verse are three couplets each illustrating one point — source or origin.

So why would Paul make this point of source or origin in this particular context? Because he is talking here about propriety. His concern is the glory of God and the testimony to unbelievers. ''So whether you eat or drink, or whatever you do, do all to the glory of God. Give no offence to Jews or to Greeks or to the church of God, just as I try to please all men in everything I do, not seeking my own advantage, but that of many, that they may be saved. Be imitators of me ...'' (1 Corinthians 10:31–11:1f RSV).

No other religion offers the feminine emancipation that Christianity offers. In Paul's day the gospel was loosing women from the appalling bondage to which they had been subject and there was the distinct danger that their freedom would hinder the gospel; hence he is requiring some concessions to social propriety for the sake of the testimony. He reminds them in chapter 10, verse 23 that whilst all things are lawful or permissible, they are not all beneficial or constructive.

In differing cultures, various parts of the physical body carry different degrees of honour or dishonour. Throughout the East, the head is the most honourable and the feet the most dishonourable, hence the significance of Paul's statement in 1 Corinthians 12:21 (RSV) ''The head [cannot say] to the feet, 'I have no need of you'.'' To the Greeks, the physical head was the seat or source of honour. By behaving dishonourably, one shamed one's own head. But the way one behaved also reflected on the person responsible for one.

Bearing in mind the pioneer nature of Paul's work in a hostile culture; bearing in mind that some sources say that husbands would be expected to divorce a wife who appeared in public improperly dressed; and bearing in mind that men were seen to be the source of respect to their wives, and that failing to honour them was seen as a disgrace — it seems reasonable to conclude that Paul was encouraging over-zealous wives to avoid the appearance of evil, even if it meant sacrificing some of their new-found freedom, and he appeals on the basis of honouring their source, just as men are to honour their source of life (Christ), and Christ honours His (God).

c) Verse 10 — power on a woman's head

What about the *exousia* on the woman's head? (1 Corinthians 11:10) It's been a gross mishandling of the passage to insert the word 'veil' as some translators have done. Increasing numbers of commentators are following the lead given by Hooker who rejects the traditional idea that the 'veil' (not even mentioned in verse 10) was a symbol of submission and argues that it means just what it says — authority over her head, i.e. the woman ought to have — be given — authority to pray, prophesy and function as a full member of the body.[19] If Paul had meant that she should have submission, he would have used the word *hupotage* (submission). He is affirming her credentials to function. Perhaps the angels, as guardians of the elect, will only be content when they see the new Eve enjoying the full fruits of salvation.

Hooker's exegesis of verse 10 leads naturally into verses 11-12. "Nevertheless, in the Lord woman is not independent of man nor man of woman; for as the woman was made from man [the point made in verse 3], so man is now born of woman. And all things are from God." This is surely the climax of Paul's argument. Hooker suggests that the 'Nevertheless' introduces the corrective to the rabbinical understanding of Genesis 2:18-22 (stated in verses 8-9).

Scholars such as Scroggs have no doubt that God is affirming the equality and mutual dependence of men and women in the Church with God as the ultimate *kephale* of all ("all things are of God"). "The climax of the *midrash* (Hebrew for 'teaching') shows men and women reunited in mutual dependence on each other and in mutual submission to God … In the eschatological community where liberation reigns, woman no longer stands chained to the subordinate roles of the old creation."[20]

d) Headcovering

What then of the headcovering issue? This was a matter of local culture given as a temporary means of expressing the principle stated — that of doing all to the glory of God and giving no offence for the gospel's sake.

Verse 5 refers to women with short hair being a disgrace. Later verses 14-15 state that nature teaches that it is a shame for a man to have long hair and a glory for women to wear hair long. Patricia Gundry says:

> But nature makes it impossible for some women to have long flowing hair. Black African women wear elaborate and twisted hairdos close to their heads because their curly hair doesn't fall long naturally. So nature here cannot mean what we think of as nature, but rather custom — what was universally considered appropriate, attractive and respectable in Corinth. It would seem natural to them.[21]

There is much debate among theologians as to whether Paul was writing about veils or hair. The exact details of custom are not really known, but the principle is surely obvious. Scroggs argues that Paul did not wish any value judgements to be drawn on the basis of sexual distinctions. What concerned the apostle was that Christians should adhere to accepted customs for distinguishing between the sexes in order to dissociate Christian worship from spurious cults which encouraged sexual perversions. He actually thinks that Paul's hidden agenda in this passage is his concern about homosexuality.[22] Murphy O'Connor's research led him to believe that long-styled hair on men was associated with homosexuality, whilst short hair could mark a woman out as a lesbian.[23]

Some will have difficulty with a hermeneutical approach which leans so strongly on the historical background to a passage. I allow F. F. Bruce to be my justifier:

> There is nothing frivolous about such an appeal to public conventions and seemliness. To be followers of the crucified Jesus was in itself unconventional enough, but needless breaches of convention were to be discouraged. A few decades later, if not as early as this, people were prepared to believe the most scandalous rumours of what went on at Christian meetings; unnecessary breaches of customary propriety would be regarded as confirmation of such rumours. It was far better to give the lie to them by scrupulous maintenance of social decorum. Though the application of the principle may vary widely, the principle itself remains valid, especially where the public reputation of the believing community is likely to depend on such externalities.[24]

Women Teaching and Exercising Authority

1 Timothy 2:8-15

The traditional interpretation of this passage is that Paul is making a clear statement forbidding women to teach or hold positions of authority over men, and that, since he is doing this with reference to the creation scriptures in Genesis, it constitutes a binding policy for all time. I believe this to be a serious misunderstanding of Paul's true meaning. When looked at apart from preconceptions, I believe this traditional view fails to make real sense of the various components in the text.

There are three exhortations in this passage:

a) to prayer (v.1),
b) to propriety in worship, and
c) to women being enabled to learn.

The third is an imperative or command whereas the others are simply present tense verbs. Paul's deepest concern here is that women be given access to learn.

This may seem an innocuous idea to us, but in the context of the first century it was frighteningly radical. The lot of women in general is summarised in Roland De Vaux's study of ancient Israel:

> The wife called her husband *Baal* or master; she also called him *adon* or lord; she addressed him, in fact, as a slave addresses his master, or a subject his king. The Decalogue includes a man's wife among his possessions, along with his house, land, his male and female slaves, his ox, his ass (Exodus 20:17; Deuteronomy 5:21). Her husband can repudiate her, but she cannot claim a divorce; all her life she remains a minor. The wife doesn't inherit from her husband, nor daughters from their father, except when there is no male heir (Numbers 27:8). A vow made by a girl or married woman needs to be validated by the consent of father or husband and if this consent is withheld, the vow is null and void. (Numbers 30:4-17). [25]

When it came to studying the law, the situation was no different. Stagg's study of women in the world of Jesus reveals, ''It was debated whether or not a man should give his daughter a knowledge of the law ... Not only was a woman not to be instructed in the law, but the rabbis made it explicit that her obligations to it were limited."[26]

"Women were not subject to education in the ancient pagan world ... Greeks did not educate their women."[27]

Jewish rabbis expressly forbade women direct access to God's law. The Talmud says, "The wise men have commanded that no man should teach his daughter the law for this reason, that the majority of them have not got a mind fitted for study, but pervert the words of the law on account of the poverty of their minds."[28]

Rabbi Eleazer added, "Let the words of the law be burned rather than given to a woman."[29] Indeed "Rabbinical prohibitions even ruled out a mother's teaching the Torah to her own children."[30]

Verse 11 is the central matter, not verse 12. Paul was offering a seed of hope for all women, which would have seemed outrageous at the time.

The word Paul chose for authority in verse 12 is actually unique in the New Testament. The word *authentein*, which carries the thought of domineering or usurping, is used rather than *exousia*, which is universally used throughout the New Testament to describe authority. Carrying as it does the idea of 'self-willed arbitrary behaviour', *authentein* is hardly legitimate for any men, let alone women.

Even more important is Paul's unusual language when he said, "I do not permit" which can equally be translated, "I am not permitting." He doesn't tell Timothy to follow his practice — he says that *he* is not allowing ... "It's descriptive, not prescriptive. An observation, not a command."[31] He could just as easily have said, "Don't allow ...", or, "They must not be permitted to ..." There are in fact a number of incidences where Paul revealed his opinions, yet we interpret them as having limited significance.[32]

Increasing numbers of biblical students are suggesting that verse 12 be seen as a parenthetical statement.[33] Not that it should be ignored, but rather seen as a statement of Paul's position, temporarily adopted until women were educated and equipped to take responsibility in the community. The fact that they were encouraged to learn in submissiveness is only relevant insofar as anyone, men or women, being taught needs to be teachable.

When interpreted this way, verses 13-15 become a basis for verse 11 (women learning), not verse 12 (prohibitions on women functioning in certain ways).

So, women should learn ... "For Adam was formed first, then Eve" (v.13). Note that he said Adam was created first *then* Eve, rather than Adam was created first, *not* Eve. The point being that Eve was also created by God, in His image, and had an equal stake in creation (cf 1 Corinthians 11:11-12). So, why shouldn't she learn the law too?

Likewise, women should learn because Eve was deceived (v.14). Learning and being instructed is one way we avoid deception; ignorance is a breeding ground for deception. The opening section of Chapter 4 is about deception and seducing spirits and Paul reminds Timothy of the good teaching he had followed (v.6), and in the same breath tells him to refuse old wives' tales (v.7). I doubt that this was a mere sexist comment — it referred to the problem all too often associated with non-educated women (and men).

Perhaps there is significance in the sequence of Genesis 2: God made Adam (v.7); He commanded him not to eat of the tree (v.17); *then* he formed Eve (v.18-22). We can assume from this that she did not hear God's command directly, but through Adam. Maybe she was ill-informed? In effect, I'm suggesting that Paul was saying, "Eve was deceived, so now women should be taught to hear God for themselves."

The notion that women should not teach, etc. because of Eve's deception is preposterous.

● Does Eve's deception in any way give grounds for the idea that all women are more susceptible to deception than men? If so,

● Does Adam's disobedience mean that all men are more susceptible to disobedience?

Since there is no logic in this argument, it would need to be clearly spelt out elsewhere, but it isn't. And experience doesn't bear it out either.

Verse 15 is odd when translated in the customary fashion. It cannot be that Paul is suggesting that Christian women will be spared pain in childbirth or guaranteed safe delivery. Surely the Amplified Bible renders it correctly: "... and they shall be saved (eternally) if they continue in faith and love and holiness through the childbearing, that is by the birth of the (divine) child.''

Paul's mind is still on Genesis, thinking of how sin came into the world through Eve. He crowns his argument for woman's emancipation by reminding us of the promise to Eve, that a Messiah would come, born of a seed of a woman, and redeem womankind (and mankind).

''… creation, the Fall and redemption all argue for woman's spiritual education. She was made, as man was, so she should learn. She gave birth to the Son of God himself as man could never do, so she is entitled to learn.''[34]

To Sum Up …

What then are the arguments against women being in leadership in the Church? Let's just mention the main points and summarise our answers.

a) That women were ordained from creation to be subordinate to men

We've shown that this was far from the case, and that there is no evidence in the Genesis passage which self-evidently shows that women should be subject to men. Conclusions in favour of subordination have to be read into the statements.

b) That man was made to be the head of the woman

'Head' as used metaphorically throughout the New Testament carries the idea of 'source' or 'origin' much more clearly than that of 'chief' or 'superior'. Other references to 'head' in the epistles lend themselves better to the idea of 'source' than 'chief'. In some cases it is used in conjunction with the preposition 'from', i.e. 'the head from whom' life flows to the rest of the body (Ephesians 4:15; Colossians 2:19). God allowed man the privilege of being the source of woman's life. But Paul balances this up by reminding us that 'in the Lord' we have interdependence (1 Corinthians 11:11-12). Men how have the opportunity to give women what they themselves have enjoyed for centuries — rights, liberties and equalities. Headship means giving and sharing what we already have — being the source of nurture, encouragement and empowerment.

There is nothing in the biblical idea of headship which prohibits women in turn being the source of leadership and ministry to men. In fact good headship on the part of men would be to give women exactly that honour.

c) That Paul forbids women having authority over men, e.g. 1 Timothy 2

Quite the reverse — seen in its historical context, this passage is Paul's argument *for* women being given the first rung of the ladder which would lead to women being equipped to teach and lead.

d) That women are not equipped for taking authority

There is nothing directly in Scripture to suggest this. There are cases of women who did lead throughout the Hebrew Scriptures, even in a culture which viewed this as taboo. For example: "I sent Moses to lead you, also Aaron and Miriam." (Micah 6:4); Deborah, who exercised authority over Barak, commander of the army; Huldah, who was a prophet (not merely one who prophesied) — she brought authoritative direction to the king and nation. As Catherine Booth observed, the authority and dignity of Huldah's message to the king betrayed none of the trembling difference or abject servility which some people seem to think should characterise the religious exercise of women.

The idea that women are not equipped to lead is shown to be nonsense in practice. In secular work, on the mission field and in churches where they have been given the opportunity, the reverse is shown to be the case.

e) That female leadership was not exercised in the New Testament

If one accepts the background argument given with reference to the 1 Timothy passage, i.e. women were untaught, this would not be surprising. But wherever women had the calling and necessary skills, they did lead.

Phoebe is first described in Romans 16:1 as a deacon (literal translation) of the church (NB not a deaconess), which is, of

course, the same term as Paul used to refer to himself,
translated 'minister'. But he then goes on to call her a 'helper'
which literally means 'to stand before' (*prostrates*). The usual
translations of the word are 'chief', 'leader of a party',
'protector' or 'champion'. Theodoret the early Church
historian notes that the fame of Phoebe was spoken of
throughout the world.

It is interesting also to note that women elders were actually
abolished around the third century, which obviously suggests
that they did exist prior to this point.

In closing I'd like to return again to F. F. Bruce's
commentary on Galatians. He develops the idea of Paul's
denial of discrimination, which is sacramentally affirmed in
the baptism formula of Galatians 3:28 and argues that it holds
good for the new existence 'in Christ' in its entirety, ''If in
ordinary life, existence in Christ is manifest openly in Church
fellowship, then, if a Gentile may exercise spiritual leadership
in Church as freely as a Jew, or a slave as freely as a citizen,
why not a woman as freely as a man?''[35]

References

1. Hayter, M. *The New Eve in Christ* (SPCK, 1982) p.3.
2. Trible, P. *God and the Rhetoric of Sexuality* (Philadelphia 1978) pp.22, 33, 69.
3. Swidler, L. *Biblical Affirmation of Women* (Philadelphia 1977) pp.31, 50 etc.
4. Jewett, P.K. *Man as Male and Female* (Eerdmans 1975) p.165.
5. Langley, M. *Equal Woman* (Marshall Pickering 1983) p.28.
6. Hayter, M. ibid. p.99.
7. Milne, B. *Know the Truth* (IVP 1982) p.131.
8. Bushnell, K. *God's Word to Women* (1923 privately reprinted) p.131.
9. Bruce, F.F. *The Epistle to the Galatians* (Exeter 1982) p.189.
10. Hayter, M. ibid. p.138.
11. Caird, G.B. *Paul and Women's Liberty* (BJRL 1971) pp.271-3.
12. Hayter, M. ibid. p.138.
13. Karris, R.J. for example, *The Role of Women According to Jesus and the Early Church*

14. Hayter, M. ibid. p.139.
15. Palmer, F.H. *New Bible Dictionary* (London 1962)
16. *The New Bible Dictionary* (IVP London 1982) p.508.
17. Bedale, S. *The Meaning of Kephale in the Pauline Epistles* (JTS new series 1954) pp.211-215.
18. Barrett, C.K. *Commentary on 1 Corinthians* (London 1971) p.248.
19. Hooker, M. *Authority on Her Head: An Examination of 1 Corinthians 11:10* (NTS 1964) p.302.
20. Scroggs, R. *Paul and the Eschatological Woman* (JAAR 1974) p.302.
21. Gundry, P. *Woman be Free* (Zondervan 1977) p.64-65.
22. Scroggs, R. ibid. p.534.
23. Murphy-O'Connor *Sex and Logic in 1 Corinthians 11:2-16* (CBQ 1980) p.485-90.
24. Bruce, F.F. *1 & 2 Corinthians* (London 1971) p.235.
25. De Vaux, R. *Ancient Israel — Its Life and Institutions* (Dartman, Longman and Todd, 1980)
26. Stagg, E.S.F. *Women in the World of Jesus* (London 1978) p.51.
27. McPheeters, J.C. *Proclaiming the New Testament: The Epistles to the Corinthians* (Baker Book House, 1964)
28. McPheeters, J.C. ibid.
29. McPheeters, J.C. ibid.
30. *New Bible Dictionary* (IVP London 1982) p.636.
31. Atkins, A. *Split Image* (Hodder and Stoughton, 1987) p.118.
32. For example:
    1 Cor. 7:7   We are not all single.
    Phmn. 10-16   We wouldn't necessarily send slaves back
                  to their masters.
    1 Tim. 5:23   We needn't all drink alcohol.
    Acts 15:29   We may eat black pudding, etc.
33. Atkins, A. e.g. ibid. p.124.
34. Atkins, A. ibid. p.123.
35. Bruce, F.F. *The Epistle to the Galatians* (Exeter 1982) p.190.

General Bibliography

Beyond Identity

Dick Keyes, Hodder and Stoughton 1984.

Beyond Sex Roles

Professor Gilbert Bilezikian, Baker Book House, 1985.

Crisis in Masculinity

Leanne Payne, Kingsway Publications, 1985.

Equal to Serve

Gretchen Gaebelein Hull, Scripture Union, 1989.

Feminine Mystique

Betty Friedman, Pelican, 1963.

Go and Make Apprentices

Phil Vogel, Kingsway Publications, 1986.

Hide & Sex

John and Christine Noble, Kingsway Publications, 1981.

Issues Facing Christians Today

John Stott, Marshalls, 1984.

Leadership Explosion

Philip King, Hodder and Stoughton, 1987.

Men, Women and God

Kathy Keay.

Split Image

Anne Atkins, Hodder and Stoughton, 1987.

The Gift of Feeling	Paul Tournier, SCM Press, 1979.
The Gospel Community	Tiller and Birchall, Marshall Pickering, 1987.
The Turning Tide	Brenda Robson, Marshall Pickering, 1989.
What in the World is God Saying about Women?	Christine Noble, Kingsway Publications, 1990.
What's Right with Feminism	Elaine Storkey, Third Way Books, SCM, 1985.
Women at the Crossroads	Kari Torjesen Malcolm, IVP, 1982.
Women in Ministry	L. E. Maxwell, Victory Books, 1987.
Women in the Bible	Mary Evans, Paternoster Press, 1983.
Women to Women	Kathy Keay.